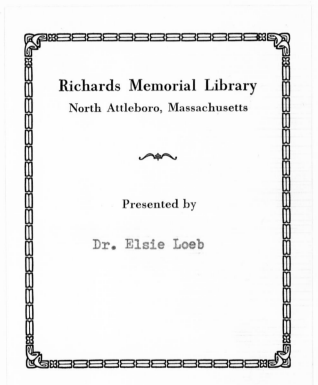

SQUIRREL
BOOK

BY EUGENE KINKEAD

Spider, Egg and Microcosm
In Every War But One
A Concrete Look at Nature
Wildness Is All Around Us
Squirrel Book

SQUIRREL BOOK

Eugene Kinkead

Illustrations by John Hamberger

E. P. Dutton • New York

Text copyright © 1980 by Eugene Kinkead
Illustrations copyright © 1980 by John Hamberger

For information contact:
Elsevier-Dutton Publishing Co., Inc.,
2 Park Avenue, New York, N.Y. 10016

Library of Congress Cataloging in Publication Data
Kinkead, Eugene
Squirrel Book
1. Gray squirrel. I. Title.
QL737.R68K56   599.32'32   80-11994

ISBN: 0-525-93137-6

Published simultaneously in Canada by
Clarke, Irwin & Company Limited,
Toronto and Vancouver

Designed by Barbara Cohen

10 9 8 7 6 5 4 3 2 1

First Edition

To the many correspondents near and far—the ardently devoted squirrel people and the equally ardent anti-squirrel people—whose numerous and sometimes multiple communications, written and oral, made this volume possible.

CONTENTS

SQUIRREL
BOOK

1. CITY SQUIRRELS

If one regards the house cat as a domesticated creature, a suggestion that may provoke argument in some quarters, then unquestionably the wild animal most familiar to Americans is the eastern gray squirrel. This frisky, adaptable, bushy-tailed imp, a fearless aerial acrobat in the treetops, as zippy as forked lightning on the ground, lives along the entire length of our eastern seaboard and westward some five hundred miles beyond the Mississippi River, penetrating to parts of the Dakotas, Nebraska, Kansas, Oklahoma, and Texas. This broad stretch of territory is home to better than three-quarters of our population of more than 220 million persons, virtually every one of whom above the age of six is acquainted with the eastern gray squirrel. To be otherwise would be impossible, for in its range the gray squirrel is ubiquitous. Impartially it inhabits rural hardwood forests, suburban groves and lawns, city parks, cemeteries, and backyards. Because of its propinquity to man, not only do millions of Americans recognize the gray squirrel, but thousands have had diverse kinds of personal experiences with it. Many of these have been surprising. Some, in fact, have been almost incredible.

1

A number of these experiences were made known to me as the result of an article I wrote for *The New Yorker* magazine on the squirrels of New York City's Central Park. For many years as I walked the park for recreation or on business as a journalist writing of nature, I had observed the squirrels. Their perky character charmed me. I marveled at their grace above ground and on it. To my secret satisfaction *The New Yorker*'s editor asked me to try an article on them. Shortly thereafter, by a stroke of good fortune, I heard that an experienced zoologist had worked intermittently for several years on a study of the squirrels in the park. He was Dr. Richard Van Gelder, a mammalogist at the American Museum of Natural History. When I asked if he could give me some facts about what he had learned, he generously agreed. My article appeared several years ago.

Readers of *The New Yorker* magazine rarely write letters about articles. Occasionally some piece or other proves an exception. Then a handful of mail may arrive. However, following publication of the item on the park squirrels, letters flowed in. They came from many states and from Canada, as well. The writers seemed anxious, almost compulsively so, to relate their experiences with squirrels, a development that surprised and also puzzled me. But the content of the communications was so interesting that the editor decided to run, some months later, a second piece on squirrels, based on the correspondence. After this appeared, the mail was even heavier. Letters came from most of the lower forty-eight states. Again Canada was represented. And this time I heard from persons in Europe and Asia. Memories of the eastern gray squirrel thus seem indelible, even in far-off places.

A plurality of the letters I received were admiring. The writers obviously esteemed the species, or at least they grudgingly recognized its achievements and the ingenuity by which they are attained. A large number of missives, on the other hand, could not be counted either pro or con; they neutrally reported an event, often an unusual one. A substantial minority, however, were openly critical. This attitude is readily comprehensible. Squirrels, for their own reasons, and for their own satisfaction, often flout the wishes of mankind. Experiences with them can be far from idyllic. Correspondents in this category tended to be grumpy or, even worse, acrimonious.

Dr. Van Gelder's interest in squirrels, I learned, was of long standing. It dated from the time he was a boy of seven, and kept one as a pet in his family's apartment in The Bronx. The association ended somewhat abruptly. The squirrel was returned to nature because of a typical antisocial act. It climbed the living-room curtains and tore them with its claws. A squirrel's claws are as sharp as a cat's, but, unlike the latter's, they are not retractable. However, they can be raised when walking so as not to dull them, an ability that is certainly useful in traversing city pavements.

Shortly after his employment at the American Museum of Natural History as a young assistant curator of mammals, Van Gelder, whose interest in squirrels had never dampened, began his study of the park animals. The museum's location made this easy. It stands on the west side of the park at Central Park West and runs from Seventy-seventh Street to Eighty-first Street. Van Gelder lived nearby. His study took place mornings and evenings when he aired his Doberman pinscher, Roulette, in the park. The two went in the entrance at Central Park West and Eighty-first Street. Walking south, they moved along the West Drive or over the terrain to the west of it, and came out through the portal at Central Park West and Seventy-seventh Street. With Roulette on her leash, Van Gelder, often to the mystification of passersby, frequently paused to observe his research subjects. Sometimes he made notes. At other times he gazed aloft into the trees. The area he worked in—Eighty-first to Seventy-seventh streets near the West Drive—comprises about one and a half acres out of the six hundred and ninety acres of land in the park. Van Gelder told me that he estimated the squirrel population in the study area to be about thirty. Many biologists consider about two squirrels to the acre in the wild to be a normal figure. "Manifestly my total is extremely high," Van Gelder said. "But there is an easy explanation. Most of the squirrels in the area I studied were to be found close to

3

the two entrances. In the park these spots have a distinct squirrel-survival value. The park squirrels get most of their food from people who feed them. It follows, then, that food is intimately connected with the volume of human traffic. This naturally is greatest around the entrances. On wet or snowy days people will come to them to feed the squirrels but would never venture into the park's interior. In inclement weather virtually no one is in the center of the park. So the heavy squirrel groupings around the entrances is a squirrel-survival technique. It's in no way indicative of the number of squirrels to be found in the park as a whole."

Shortly after this talk, in order to get an idea of the actual number of the park's squirrels, I took a census. I, too, discovered them to be thickest around the site's fifty-two entrances. The exception was in the northern section, where there are twenty entrances. The land there verges on Harlem and on neighborhoods generally less affluent than those farther south. Despite the presence of a seemingly ideal habitat for squirrels in the lordly woods crowning Great Hill, they were noticeably scarce all through this area. The only tenable explanation, I concluded, was that the people nearby had other uses for their time and money than buying and distributing fodder for squirrels.

When I had finished the census, I calculated the park's squirrel community at something more than four hundred individuals. Whatever the precise tally was, Van Gelder thought it was two or three times larger than would be the case without people feeding the squirrels.

Had Van Gelder been able to complete his study doubtless a good deal more would be known about city squirrels than is today. To begin with, Van Gelder had the sensible notion of seeking help from other park dog-walkers. His idea was to pass out mimeographed maps. The recipients could then aid him by returning them marked with the number and location of squirrels they saw in the park. But the program never got off the ground. Even after considerable publicity in the newspapers about the Van Gelder squirrel study, dog-walkers in the park took a disinterested view of combining pet exercise with squirrel enumeration.

Secondly, Van Gelder, with a scientist's understandable desire for specifics, wished to mark individual squirrels with different colored dyes shot from a water pistol. This would allow him to identify them, trace their movements, and total their numbers. A special Parks Department license would, in all probability, have been necessary for such an operation. But, even if he had been able to get one, Van Gelder, after some thought, decided that brandishing a pistol in the park, even a water pistol, was likely to be misinterpreted by nervous strollers. Finally, he was at this time appointed acting chairman of the museum's department of mammalogy, and his work load increased. So the study, after a run of several years, ended.

Although incomplete, the research produced findings beyond the determination that squirrels clustered around park entrances. The data revealed how cannily and triumphantly park squirrels had adapted to city life. As Van Gelder's work made clear, the lives of park squirrels and of wild squirrels were very different. One example is the fearlessness of park squirrels. In the wild, it is practically impossible to approach a squirrel without its seeking shelter. Hunters are well aware of this. A woodlands squirrel instinctively keeps a tree trunk or branch between itself and the gunner. Central Park squirrels, belying wild forebears that inhabited the pre-park site a century ago, intrepidly approach and badger park visitors, almost demanding food. Similar boldness is characteristic of city squirrels in general, while those of suburbia also show little fear of man. During his study, Van Gelder watched more than one park squirrel crouch practically nose to nose with Roulette, straining at her leash, as it waited for some tidbit to be thrown. City squirrels have long ago accustomed themselves to leashed dogs; in essence, they sneer at them.

In the forests gray squirrels prefer hickory nuts, hazelnuts, and the acorns of the white oak to fruits of other trees. Scientists in the past have observed them going to some length to satisfy these pref- 5 erences. In the city, however, this is not so. During his research, Van Gelder tried setting down rows of mixed nuts, preferred and non-preferred, before squirrels to note their choices. Invariably the experimentees acted much more like taste-dulled, citified, fast-food addicts than traditional squirrel gourmets; they simply grabbed the nearest nut and made off with it. In surroundings of urban sophistication, city squirrels, as might be expected, also consume victuals not normally found in the woodlands. Some items recorded on their metropolitan bill of fare are bagels, Cheetos, Cracker Jacks, Fritos, pancakes, peanut-butter crackers, pizza, and popcorn. Feeders have noted that all go down with equal relish.

In addition to the exotic provender that is the gift of human friends, city squirrels on their own supply themselves with snacks out of the ordinary, aided by the equipment and unmitigated cheek that nature has given them. Four long functional toes, ending in claws, are on front paws; the fifth member is a vestigial thumb. The arrangement enables the squirrel to use its forepaws like hands. It manipulates objects of manageable size rapidly and so dextrously that rarely does it let one fall. Therefore activities that are unusual for a four-footed animal can be undertaken and successfully completed. One of these is poaching candy from vending machines. Squirrels, like dogs, have a taste for sweets. Apparently cats do not or do so only rarely; most authorities feel cats lack an interest in sweets either through an inability to taste them or a dislike of the taste. Squirrels, on the other hand, have often shown a fondness for candy. In Pittsburgh's Schenley Park, for instance, one was seen regularly to reach a forepaw up into the back of an outdoor vending machine, pull out a candy bar, and run away and eat it. (He preferred bars with nuts.) At Duke University more or less the same thing happened. A squirrel somehow got into a dormitory and robbed another vending machine of candy and nuts.

The most common and non-exotic food given city squirrels, especially in parks, is peanuts. In Central Park, for example, visitors buy bags of peanuts from vendors in or near the park, and scatter the contents over the ground for the squirrels. The squirrels appear grateful and gobble them up, but it is questionable whether such a diet is good for them. Van Gelder suspected that some fur loss and poor eyesight that he detected among park squirrels was caused by overconsumption of peanuts. Earlier, the naturalist Ernest Thompson Seton had the same criticism of a peanut diet. In parks that he visited not long after the turn of the century, he noted the same effects as Van Gelder. If indeed the charge is valid, the diet deficiency in city squirrels may be at least partly offset by more natural foodstuffs. They, along with others of their kind in forests and suburbia, crop tree foliage in the spring. In Central Park, when the growing season starts, I have often walked under a rain of tiny twigs dropped from above by squirrels that have eaten the buds, young leaves, or

blooms. The animal holds the cut twig between its proficient fore-paws, rotating it to nibble off the flowers or leaves, then lets it fall. In the autumn park squirrels, despite handouts, also consume acorns.

Whatever the food ingested, squirrels, whether in the woods or town, need water, fresh and abundant, once or twice a day. In Central Park, I have seen a squirrel perch on the edge of the beaver pool in the park's zoo and take deep draughts under the quiet gaze of the cage's immersed occupants, the largest representatives of the rodent family in North America (the squirrel is a smaller member of the rodent family). Since the squirrel remains active in winter, it takes its water at that time of year where it can find it. This may be in the form of snow or perhaps rainwater held in the pockets of trees. But it is also inventive in making water where there is none. In Timonium, Maryland, for example, when a squirrel found the water frozen in its habitual drinking trough, it sat down on the ice until it melted. Then it wheeled and drank its fill. In the spring squirrels love to swig sweet maple sap. They nip the ends off maple shoots and sit for minutes contentedly lapping the oozing liquid. On cold nights, when the drippings freeze, the squirrel is there next morning to chew off the icicles.

Urbanization has drastically altered the pattern of the city squirrel's life. In the wild, the gray is customarily active only during the hours of lesser light—in other words, the hours of early morning and late afternoon to early evening. In this way, it is possible in mixed forest areas for it to be part of a population of four species of squirrels. Besides the gray, these are the flying, the fox, and the red squirrel. The flying, the only nocturnal species, is a beautiful little creature, overall only ten inches long; it "flies" by gliding from tree to tree by means of outstretched folds of skin that extend between the ankles of the fore and hind legs. The fox squirrel, the largest of the quartet, more than two feet long, lives amid hardwood trees, as does the gray. But it is active during the bright midday hours when the gray is not. The red, the noisiest of the four, a constant chatterer, measures up to fourteen inches long, being smaller than the gray, whose average length is eighteen inches. The red squirrel dwells among the evergreens. Thus each species occupies a separate ecological niche. There is no overlapping. All, at least in theory, can dwell peaceably together. In actuality, this is sometimes difficult, especially with the red squirrel, who is cantankerous to an extreme. Often neither man nor beast can come within its sight and escape a sound tongue lashing.

All four species have notably large tails, but the gray is deemed to have unquestionably the largest and most conspicuous. Half its length is taken up by what is, relatively speaking, the most lavish and magnificent tail borne by any furry quadruped.

In the forest, the gray squirrel wakes at the crack of dawn. Food and water are on its mind. At first, it is silent, limbering up slowly before setting out to forage. However, as the sun rises and it sights one or two others of its kind, it grows livelier. It may then dash about the treetops in frolicsome play—eight hops and a pause over long branches. Or it may make the woods ring with a lively call. The qua-qua-qua-qua-qua-a-a is repeated over and over, the vocalist all the while, however, keeping an alert eye for foes. Sounds other than this are in its repertoire, too. It chides quack-quack; it purrs, softly catlike, with pleasure; it buzzes when angry; chatters its teeth as a warning; and has, as well, a distinct and varied song that is a combination of loud and soft, not unpleasant noises. In suburbia's outback, where squirrels may act much like forest creatures, a resident wrote me that he was awakened in the early morning by squirrel music from a nearby hickory. Perched beside the minstrel, raptly attentive, were half a dozen English sparrows. From time to time, one of the feathered audience added a few chirrups of its own.

Even before mid-morning has arrived, however, the forest gray slips without fanfare back to its nest, where it remains until late afternoon. Then the search for food and drink is renewed, this time, though, softly. Usually as twilight approaches there are few sounds to be heard other than the overhead rustle of twigs or the patter of small feet on fallen leaves. The early-morning and late-afternoon periods of low-intensity light are normally the woods squirrel's only spells of activity, but occasional wanderings occur when the moon is full and the sky is clear. Such outings, however, are fraught with peril. Owls, which relish squirrels, are abroad then.

By contrast, the city squirrel has no such rigid twice-a-day schedule. It rises when it feels like it; it retires likewise. Throughout the entire day it is active. The bright midday hours, so beloved of the

fox squirrel and shunned by its country cousin, mean nothing to it. I have seen a pair in Central Park climb head downward into a wire wastebasket to retrieve some sandwich scraps from a discarded lunchbag shortly after high noon. Predators here differ, too. In the forest, these are wild things—the aforementioned owls; hawks; those tree-climbing members of the weasel family, the marten and fisher; wildcats; foxes; and tree-ascending snakes. Perhaps the last is the squirrel's deadliest foe, especially to nests of young. One of my correspondents has written indignantly, "A snake, god damn it, can climb anything—anywhere." I must say I was dubious about this statement until a few months ago. Then a snake, not a very large or powerful one, measuring perhaps two feet in length, emerged from my bathroom floor cabinet under the wash basin when I opened the cabinet door. It had ascended the smooth copper tubing from the pipes in the basement three stories below, and entered the enclosure through a generous hole the plumber had bored in the floor. The site from which it came was the Connecticut countryside surrounding my home.

In the city, of course, the squirrel has no such enemies. The wild things have all been suppressed. But there are other dangers. Feral cats can make a play for squirrels as certainly as unleashed dogs do. Children as well sometimes give chase. My experience has been that none of these pose a serious threat. For years I have seen onrushing dogs in Central Park easily avoided by squirrels. The squirrel makes a quick turn or dashes up a tree, seemingly rather enjoying the sport. Cats are more threatening, but the squirrels I have watched have no difficulty in detecting their stalk and evading it, the while roundly reviling the pursuer. Children, of course, would only be sorry if they laid hands on a squirrel, but I've never seen even the swiftest or most persistent come even as close as a dog. However, there is one principal and much-feared urban enemy, the automobile. Considering its leadership in the industry, General Motors Corporation may be the city squirrel's most successful predator. Certainly the quarry itself 11 has become inordinately wary of the company's products, as well, to be sure, as those of other makers.

The treed turf of several acres that surrounds the American Museum of Natural History is officially called Roosevelt Park, and Van Gelder was puzzled at the relatively large number of squirrels he saw there in the daytime. He had found several nests in the park's trees, but their capacity was certainly insufficient to account for the quantity of squirrels he saw. The site couldn't, he felt, be the permanent home for all of them. The mystery remained a mystery for many months. Then Van Gelder arrived early at the museum one morning after a light overnight snowfall. The riddle was solved. Squirrel paw prints dotted the snow on Central Park West where the traffic was still sparse. The squirrels, recognizing their enemy, had crossed from Central Park just after dawn. They returned the same way, before motorists were up and about.

But this is only one instance of metropolitan squirrel savvy. Other cases from all over New York tell of auto-shy and traffic-wise squirrels. And my letters indicate the same is true of other urban areas. Squirrels inhabit all those New York City parks that have a few trees. One of them, Stuyvesant Square Park, in lower Manhattan on the East Side, has a good-sized squirrel community. The fairly extensive plot is divided by the broad pavement of Second Avenue. Car movement over it is brisk, but doesn't endanger the squirrels. A regular visitor states that when squirrels wish to get from one half of the park to the other they wait patiently on the sidewalk until the city's traffic control system halts the vehicular flow. Then they zoom across in safety. The same is true further uptown at Madison Square Park, whose western border is Fifth Avenue. To safely raid a bird-feeding station that existed at the foot of a statue across Fifth Avenue some years back, the squirrels in the square waited for the avenue to clear. As a final note in this connection, let me insert a letter I received. The stationery was headed: MEYER DAVIS' MUSIC, Orchestras Extraordinary. The message:

Believe it or not, this morning I saw a squirrel beside
the West Drive in Central Park wait for the green light to
turn red before crossing the road.

Sincerely,
Meyer Davis

The creature being discussed here, whether of forest or town, is
a smallish mammal. As an adult in the northern part of its range, it
may attain a length of twenty inches; in the southern, the maximum
is more apt to be seventeen inches. The basic normal color anywhere, when glimpsed at a distance, is light gray. On closer inspection, the fur shows white underparts. There is short yellowish hair
on the face and muzzle, and white tips to the guard hairs. Four large
incisors for cutting are the most prominent teeth, accompanied by
six premolars and twelve molars for chewing. Ears are small, triangular, and usually erect; the whiskers long, black, and pointed. Male
and female are about the same size, the female being every bit as
strong and active as the male. Individuals ordinarily tip the scale at
about a pound, but a female that is perhaps the largest specimen on
record went a pound and a half. Much of the weight is concentrated
in the large, powerful hind-leg muscles.

The squirrel's senses are well-developed. Two of the more important, however, sight and smell, seem to have odd limitations. The
squirrel can see at a great distance, perhaps farther than any rodent.
Probably this is because it dwells high in the trees. These are often
leafless, and sighting enemies from afar is desirable. However, food
lying on the ground near a squirrel is often overlooked. Many who
wrote me have noticed this. One correspondent is an old friend,
Miss Cynthia Westcott. She was long known in certain nature circles
as The Plant Doctor. In Glen Ridge, New Jersey, for many years, she
conducted a successful botanical rescue service for all kinds of ailing
garden flora. Now retired to Croton-on-Hudson, New York, she
wrote me concerning nearby squirrel vision as follows: 13

"Each autumn the squirrels around here make a nest in the tulip tree across the way. Last fall they started late, when most of the leaves in their own tree were gone. They jumped to the oak next door, took a leaf stem in the mouth, and jumped several feet *up* to the very fine twigs on the tulip tree. They never missed. But they seem to have poor eyesight for close things such as a nut lying on the ground. A bluejay perched on top of a tree, for instance, will spy the nut and descend to grab it quicker than the squirrel two feet away."

With the sense of smell, squirrels seem to reverse the peculiarity present in sight. Smell is keen when objects are near, but not when distant. For example, they easily detect through their sense of smell nuts that have been buried. Burial of nuts, as everybody knows, is an important feature of squirrel husbandry. Besides finding nuts underground, squirrels are able to locate and uncover other buried food such as flower bulbs below as much as six inches of earth. And from England comes another instance of the ability to sniff out close-up goodies. A cyclist, whose lunch was in a leather attaché case tied to the rack behind the seat, parked his machine on the street to do an errand. In his absence, a descendant of our grays, which were introduced into Great Britain years ago, smelled the sandwiches within, chewed through the leather, and ate them. But here is the peculiarity. The squirrel, of course, is a game animal. Unlike such a fellow game animal as a deer, however, it cannot recognize approaching enemies through odor. Hunters know this. They can, if they are stealthy enough, close in on a squirrel upwind without its being aware.

Hearing is obviously sharp. The snap of a twig or the scuffling of leaves on the ground instantly alerts squirrels. Touch seems adequate, too. The whiskers, sensitive as a cat's, inform the squirrel whether a hole will, or will not, permit entry. Other useful tactile hairs an inch or more long are near the eye and under the chin. The squirrel dislikes and shuns the sticky material that some persons daub on the boles of trees to discourage its presence.

14   Very little study up to now has been made of its sense of taste.

But when pet squirrels are fed an assortment of items not normally found in nature, they accept some and reject others, indicating an effective ability to distinguish flavors.

Far and away the squirrel's most notable physical characteristic is its long, full, and undulating tail. Even squirrel detractors give it grudging praise. "The rat with the beautiful tail" is sometimes their pejorative identification. An old yarn gives this account of how it happened. The squirrel in the Garden of Eden was horrified at the sight of Adam and Eve eating the apple. It pulled its tail, then a far more ordinary member, across its eyes to hide the perfidy. As a reward, God gave it its present magnificent appendage.

The adornment, so splendid, so dramatic, is also highly useful. It serves as a sunshade; as a blanket in cold or stormy weather; as an expressive aid to communication, the tempo of its ripples indicating the depth of emotion being expressed; as a counterbalance in effecting marvelously quick turns; as an aerial rudder when its owner leaps from branch to branch, and as a parachute to soften the impact of occasional falls. On sunlit summer noons, the squirrel arches its tail over its head like a parasol; in the dead of winter the animal does not hibernate, but the tail is wrapped around the curled-up form in the nest like a comforter, preserving body heat. Males can be seen flicking it in skirmishes that interrupt their pursuit of females over the bare limbs of trees in late February or early March; it is employed as a foil against their rivals the way a bullfighter uses his cape to befuddle the bull.

One indication of the importance of the tail is the time the owner spends in grooming and fluffing it. All bits of foreign matter are sedulously removed. One of the most intent and unhappy squirrels I have ever seen was sitting on the low limb of a tree on Summit Rock, the highest point in Central Park. It was trying, in obvious desperation, to remove with claws and teeth some chewing gum that had become embedded in its tail.

Throughout the winter, squirrels forage actively and, since winter life in Central Park is less rigorous than in the woodlands, park 15

squirrels generally have an easier time of it in cold weather than their country counterparts. However, both are subjected to ice storms, when the branches of trees are glazed with frozen rain. These storms make for perilous footing aloft. More than once in Central Park I have seen squirrels fall to the ground while trying to make progress along ice-coated tree limbs. On these occasions, the tail swings rapidly from side to side, gripping the air somewhat in the manner of a parachute. Furthermore, the legs are spread. The loose skin of the body then stretches to become an abbreviated form of the gliding apparatus of the flying squirrel. Without exception, in my experience, the tumbling squirrel upon hitting the ground picks himself up and makes off, none the worse for the mishap.

The preservative functions of the tail and loose skin were undoubtedly exercised in what is perhaps the longest nonfatal squirrel drop from a building on record. It occurred July 19, 1934. On that morning, Mr. and Mrs. Clyde Cooper, of Memphis, checked into the Hotel Lincoln in New York City for rest after an all-night drive. The room clerk noted they were accompanied by a pet squirrel which they said they were taking south to their son, Billy. In their room on the sixteenth floor, the travelers retired, the couple to bed and the squirrel to a towel spread for it on a chair. Not long afterward, an office crew in the accounting department on the third floor some sixty feet below the guest's room heard a thud in a nearby airshaft. At the bottom of this they found the squirrel, which had either fallen or jumped from an open window in the Cooper's quarters. It was stunned, so they picked it up and summoned a veterinarian. He noted that the squirrel had suffered a slight nosebleed, but predicted that it would soon be all right. Sure enough, by four o'clock that afternoon the pet was frolicking about the Cooper's room.

A reader referred me to an even more remarkable instance of survival from a fall. The incident was reported by the naturalist, John Burroughs, who quoted the account of a traveler in Mexico. The traveler had seen two boys capture a large squirrel that they believed

to be bewitched. The squirrel at first got away. In trying to avoid pursuit by the boys, it scaled a large pine and leaped sixty feet from it to land unharmed on the roof of a house. There the boys caught it again and placed it in a pillow slip. They took this to the edge of a crag overlooking the valley of a river whose floor was six hundred feet below. On the crag the pillow slip was opened. The squirrel had the option of remaining in it or leaping out into the air above the valley. It chose the latter. It leapt. The reader states that "it fluttered rather than fell into the abyss below. The legs began to move like those of a swimming poodle dog, but quicker and quicker, while the tail, slightly elevated, spread out like a feather fan." The squirrel, in time, landed on a rock ledge a distant, visible form in the open, tree- 19 less area. After a bit, it was seen to squat there on its hind legs and smooth its ruffled fur. Then, without any apparent discomfort, it hopped down to the river.

One naturalist has stated that a squirrel can survive any fall. In light of the above, this generality does not seem entirely implausible.

Besides leaving Central Park for the natural history museum's grounds to the west, the park squirrels also migrate eastward across Fifth Avenue to a large plot of planted ground at Ninetieth Street. This is the garden of the old Andrew Carnegie mansion, now the property of the Cooper-Hewitt Museum. Some time ago I spoke with the caretaker, Manuel Perez, who had been at the place for forty years, the first twelve while it was still the home of the steel magnate's widow. The garden has grass, flower beds and several large trees, with benches interspersed to let people sit outside. Along the street perimeter it is surrounded by a high ornamental iron fence backed by stout wire mesh. "We have always had Central Park squirrels coming in and out," Perez told me. "They climb right up and down the fence with no trouble at all. People in the garden give them nuts. They take the nuts and run up the trees with them."

Central Park squirrels have occasionally gone further afield into the city's stony corridors. During his study, Van Gelder wondered whether some squirrels might not be commuting between Central Park and other city parks, such as Riverside Park, four blocks to the west. There is some evidence that they are. One afternoon Van Gelder followed a squirrel leaving the museum grounds going west along West Seventy-seventh Street. It crossed Columbus Avenue and was halfway to Amsterdam Avenue when he lost sight of it among sidewalk pedestrians. "It may have eventually made its way across Broadway and West End Avenue and on to Riverside Park," Van Gelder said. "My guess is that's where it was going." Although Van Gelder's statement was a speculation, it's indeed a fact that squirrels might move to very odd places in the city by routes its human residents have probably never considered.

One such squirrel, who almost certainly came originally from

Central Park, was the subject a few years back of a newspaper account, in which the writer expressed puzzlement at a squirrel's oft-proved ability to emerge at unexpected points and to meet and best unusual situations. The report said that workers in offices back of the Three Crowns Restaurant on East Fifty-fourth Street just off Fifth had been losing man-hours in engrossed mystification at the doings of a vagabond gray squirrel that had set up housekeeping somewhere in the restaurant's rear wall. The writer went on: "Squirrels are rare a quarter of a mile south of Central Park, probably because of the heavy traffic and poor foraging, but this adventurous member of the breed waxes fat on heaven knows what diet." At the time of the appearance of the item, the squirrel had been ensconced on the premises a full fortnight.

The origin of the next squirrel may, or may not, have been Central Park, but its presence in unexpected surroundings shows the interest, and sometimes the concern, that people have for this fellow resident of the city. A letter from one of my correspondents begins:

"This Sunday morning I was having breakfast at the little luncheonette on the corner of First Avenue and Fiftieth Street when I noticed a crowd gathered outside the window all looking at something perched in a small tree. Going out I found everyone was staring at a waspish little squirrel huddled on a branch. Everyone wondered where it came from and how it had gotten to this thickly populated part of town, and everyone was worried that it might get run over or attacked by the East Side dogs and cats, whose number is legion.

"I finally called the Society for the Prevention of Cruelty to Animals. Though it was Sunday, a cheerful, intelligent voice answered and said not to worry. The squirrel probably had its home in a larger tree nearby and had wandered to the small tree around dawn. As for the dogs or cats, I need not worry for the little squirrel could move like lightning and would get back to its nest safely."

That First Avenue squirrel did manage to create a bit of turmoil, but probably the greatest squirrel brouhaha that New York City has ever known came from a squirrel clearly identified as coming from 21

Central Park. The occasion began early on a June morning some years back. The escapee during its course paid an extended visit to a large area of the East Side, whose occupants throughout were notably exercised. Furthermore, they knew whom to call about the progress of the voyager. The squirrel was first seen proceeding across Fifth Avenue to Sixtieth Street. There it continued up Sixtieth to Madison Avenue, then on to Park Avenue. It advanced by way of the pavement, street trees, and town-house balconies, producing as it went a rash of telephone calls to authorities at the Central Park Zoo. Eventually a keeper was sent in pursuit. But despite his best efforts he was unable to retrieve the rover. By the next day it had made its way to Lexington Avenue and Fifty-ninth Street. This is one of the city's busiest intersections. Bloomingdale's department store stands there, and across the street are many smaller shops. Here, scampering gaily over store awnings, the squirrel collected a traffic-blocking crowd. The assemblage was soon augmented by four hastily summoned policemen. Armed with heavy sacks, the officers spent an extremely active half hour pursuing their quarry. At each near seizure and escape, the crowd cheered lustily. Finally, after an outstanding bit of encirclement, the squirrel was bagged by Patrolman Mendotity, who headed for Central Park and carried the wanderer back to its native heath.

2. MORE ON CITY SQUIRRELS

Forest squirrels, unlike city ones, tenant only three types of homes. The most permanent is the den, a hollow in a tree, formed when a branch three inches or more in diameter dies through shade-out, lightning strike, disease, or other cause. Depending on the species, ten to thirty years may pass before the limb drops off and the heartwood behind it turns to pulp. The squirrel removes the rot and lines the cavity with soft materials. Females use dens for rearing families. Dens also provide snug winter quarters, and adult males are allowed in then. A large den in cold weather can accommodate as many as eight to twelve of the sociable creatures, with, usually, a nucleus of family members, the young of the year normally staying with the mother through the winter. The den, in either a dead or a live tree, is preferably fifty or sixty feet above the ground. In the case of a live tree, the den may afford squirrels a home for half a century. The occupants gnaw back the bark that attempts to grow over the entry.

The next best roof over a wild squirrel's head is the more substantial of two kinds of leaf nests, both of which are waterproof and both of which are sometimes called drays. The more substantial nest, 23 like its less permanent counterpart, resembles a ball of leaves about two feet in diameter, and is used both as litter nest and winter shelter when den sites are unavailable. Located high in a tree or securely anchored in a crotch, it is constructed on a platform of woven branches and twigs. Inside is a cavity about six inches in diameter lined with such soft items as shredded bark, moss, grass, ferns, and sedges. Overhead twigs and leaves are laid and interlaced so as to bar the weather. The entrance is at the side.

The more loosely built variety of leaf nest is fashioned for summer occupancy only, usually by a male, who takes no part in family duties. He rests there during the hot midday hours, a typical example of masculine indolence. I have sometimes fantasized the creature idly turning the pages of *Playboy*. However, all is not invariably beer and skittles for the lounger. An authority has stated that he has seen hawks that, upon spying the flimsy treetop ball, swoop down upon it and rise with a squirrel in their talons.

City squirrels, on the other hand, can almost never acquire a den. An excess over the years of untended trees is necessary for the rotting process. But, in any case, there is some evidence that even if dens were available, city squirrels would prefer a substitute. These are specially built squirrel shelters. Some of them, highly patronized, still existed in Central Park during Van Gelder's study, the remains of a dozen or more that had been constructed and put up a few years earlier. The initiator was a refugee from Nazi Germany who resided in the city at the time and frequently visited the park. She was of the unshakable opinion that the squirrels suffered cruelly in cold or stormy weather, and should be supplied with enlarged versions of wooden birdhouses in which to keep cozy and warm. She demanded these lodgings of park authorities on pain of exposing them in letters to the newspapers as heartless abusers of animals. Her particular target was the horticulturist for the borough of Manhattan, an amiable man named Cornelius O'Shea, whose assistants regularly ascended trees for pruning and other duties. Soon, because Mr.

O'Shea was an obliging and kindly Irishman, they were also affixing squirrel houses to tree branches. Squirrels crowded into them. Below one of these near Eighty-first Street and Central Park West, Van Gelder once stood and coaxed out of it with a clucking food call a total of sixteen squirrels, which circled in a line expectantly down the bole toward him. Visitors near him were amazed.

At the time of my article, only a few of the structures remained. Two were in the Ramble, the heavily wooded hill area southeast of the museum, where they were once fairly common. These and others are monitored by self-appointed squirrel guardians. A while back a woman inquired of the horticulturist's office about a house that was missing from a beech near the statue of Wladyslaw Jagiello, the fifteenth-century Polish king, which stands in the middle of the park, east of Belvedere Lake. When the house reappeared after rehabilitation, she telephoned her gratitude to those responsible.

The refugee from Nazi Germany long ago returned to her homeland. Probably few, if any, of the structures she inspired remain, because of the ravages of time and weather and the lack of a forceful advocate. Park squirrels today are forced to do what some of them had been doing all along—find or create nests of their own. They hole up in whatever suitable tree hollows are to be found in the park, and they build both kinds of drays. I once found a good example of the more permanent form of dray sitting about thirty-five feet from the ground in the crotch of a red oak a few yards in from Fifth Avenue at Sixty-seventh Street. Later, during my census walk, I watched a squirrel scamper up to it bearing a bit of cloth, which presumably it was going to put in the nest cavity. It was doubtless a female, and she carried the cloth the way she would transport one of her babies, by tucking it against her chest and lowering her chin.

Squirrels take nest-lining very seriously. Part of a letter from a gentleman told of a tea that he took on his hostess's lawn. It was in a Detroit suburb one spring afternoon. Suddenly the lady grew vocal and excited! "Crazy, crazy, crazy!" she said, gazing out across the lawn. "Look at that demented squirrel stripping the cedar bark from that rustic seat." Sure enough, a squirrel was peeling bark from the 25 furniture. "I told her," my correspondent wrote, "that the squirrel was probably a female, acquiring some nesting material. The natural odor of the cedar would probably diminish the number of nest vermin, too." Keepers of cemeteries, sites much frequented by city squirrels, are often mystified, while members of patriotic societies all over the country are rendered indignant at the disappearance of small flags set out to decorate graves. The cloth is used for nest linings. In addition, city squirrels establish handy *pieds-à-terre* wherever they can. The locations would doubtless astonish their wild brothers. They turn nooks and crannies of any city building into lodgings. I have seen several during a pelting rain crouching contentedly in the space between the sills and old-fashioned air conditioners jutting from the windows of the museum across from Central Park.

Breeding's first cycle occurs in the winter, the farther north in the range the later. As in much of nature, the male is ready before the female, his hormonal activity customarily antedating hers by several weeks. The male begins to show an active interest in the opposite sex, but if the female isn't receptive, that fact is quickly imparted to the suitor by a few informatory nips. In the area of New York City, mating starts well before the spring equinox. In Central Park I have watched males racing over leafless branches in late February and early March in eager quest of consorts. This leads to some scuffling, of course, during which the tail comes into play as a foil. But little serious combat results. Supremacy usually is soon established and the female, acceding to the life principle's salutary tradition, accepts the stronger and more aggressive swain.

During mating a waxy plug, which seals the vagina, follows entry of the sperm, and keeps it in place until the female ovulates, which is shortly thereafter. Gestation then begins. The waxy substance secreted by the male has another purpose—it preserves the scent of urine in territorial markings. Otherwise this would disappear quickly with weathering. Not a great deal is known about squirrel territorial marking but, as is the case with most mammals, it is doubtless important. Those spots on trees where the bark is chewed off either for food, tooth reduction, or territorial marking often have spots of squirrel urine beside them. Secretion from glands at the corners of the mouth may also identify the chewer for the information of other squirrels. In addition, both males and females have been seen to drag their rears along branches. All this undoubtedly is for the purpose of indicating territory. The whole phenomenon of leaving scent to denote occupancy is apparently an important part of squirrel life.

Gestation takes six and a half weeks. In late March or early April, in the New York City area, the babies are born. Usually they are three or four in number, but squirrel litters can range in size from two to five. At birth, the young are hairless except for a few tiny whisker points. Slightly more than an ounce in weight and an inch in length, they are blind, and their ears are only tightly folded flaps. The mother, capable and affectionate, nurses and licks them industriously. In a week, they have doubled their weight and almost doubled their length. During the second week, hair starts to push through the skin of the back. In three weeks the lower incisors erupt, followed a week later by the upper ones. These are the animal's most formidable teeth, very sharp and strong. In adults, the upper incisors are about a quarter of an inch long and the lower more than half an inch. After five weeks, the eyes open and the triangular ears have already risen and taken shape. A week later, the molars begin to push through the gums. In the adult, these teeth have crowns with low cusps, adapted for crushing seeds, nuts, roots, and other vegetable matter. They do a highly efficient job. Food particles are ground so fine that differentiation of the contents of a squirrel's stomach is a near-to-impossible task. At six weeks the young can take solid food. Weaning begins then, but nursing continues for another month and a half. With opened eyes, the young start taking an interest in the world outside. Very cautiously they emerge from the nest and, staying close to its entrance, they eat tree flowers, buds, or young leaves. In another fortnight, they are almost half grown and fully furred.

The mother keeps them so well groomed that their coats literally shine. The fur smells, says one researcher, like a freshly opened hickory nut.

Now the young scamper around the bole of the home tree, using a different gait than the one most frequently employed on the ground. In circling a tree, a squirrel moves all four legs separately instead of the front and hind legs in pairs as it does when it hops, its usual gait on terra firma.

The young customarily stay with the mother for from twelve to thirty weeks, or longer. Sometimes squirrels have two litters a year, especially in the south. (On the other hand, if food is scarce in the area, all breeding may be omitted altogether, another precept from nature's sensible book of rules.) If there's a second litter, it arrives in midsummer and the mother leaves the first brood after twelve weeks and moves to another nest, whose young stay with her through the winter. Otherwise, the young of the first and only brood get that privilege. Whichever is the case, however, young and mother part company the next spring. Full growth is attained by the youngsters in two years. Mating, however, may start earlier than that.

Sometimes a squirrel uses two nests for one brood. Ordinarily the female prepares the second nest for an emergency, which is usually the presence of nest vermin or threat by a predator. The nests may be yards apart. When young sucklings are menaced by a predator, their mouths are so fashioned that the mother can retreat with them hanging to her teats after the manner of a mother mouse. When the young are larger, transport is always done in the same way. With a few notes of warning, the mother readies the youngsters for the move. Using her incisors, she takes firm hold of the belly skin of the first. At this, without a moment's delay, the baby places its small fore and hind legs securely about her neck so that it can hold tight. Its tail is tucked out of harm's way by being bent up over the parent's back. It is then held snugly by pressure from the mother's chin. With safety and convenience thus achieved, the mother is off

like a shot. A researcher reported that in twelve minutes a mother

cleared the nest of several young, placing them in another nest a
hundred yards away.

Although the dominant squirrel of a neighborhood is always a
large male, dominant or not, he avoids a mother's nest. A mother
squirrel is every bit the physical equal of a male. Unless resistance is
futile, as in the case of an overwhelmingly powerful predator, she is
valiant in defense of her nest; although sometimes against en-
croachers from whom she might reasonably be expected to flee, she
fights. Dr. Vagn Flyger, one of the country's better-known squirrel

experts, tells this of a colleague: "While he was into a nest to examine some babies, the mother returned. She was so furious that she ran up his leg, out along his arm, and nipped his thumb." Underlining this behavior is a paragraph from the writings of Dr. F. S. Barkalow, another squirrel authority:

"Mother squirrels are brave in coming to the rescue when their young cry for help. Until it is about three and one half months old, the nestling has a piercing squeal which brings its mother running. Investigators handling young squirrels should keep a wary eye on the branches above. Biologists Hans Uhlig and Gordon Clark have each been bitten by a female gray squirrel turned tigress."

As brave as she is in defense of her offspring, the mother is equally solicitous in case of accident. Herewith an example. In its first attempt to climb about a tree, a young squirrel lost its hold and dropped twenty feet to the ground. Without the aerial finesse possessed by adults, it fell like a log and lay stunned and helpless. The agitated mother rushed down the tree and nosed it over anxiously. When it began to stir, she gripped its belly skin soundly and carried it, clinging about her neck, back to the safety of the nest.

Squirrel mothers are dedicated teachers. Nor do they brook nonsense. A lady in Texas who raised four baby squirrels with unopened eyes through milk dispensed from a medicine dropper when she was a child of nine wrote me as follows:

"Have you ever seen a mother squirrel making her baby take his first trip across the high telephone wire? It's heart-rending. Baby creeps close. He puts his forepaws around her neck. It's too hard a task, he says. She backs off firmly. No coddling here. She stays several feet ahead, now chattering in a shrill no-nonsense sort of tone. Baby teeter-totters, making a whining chatter. He inches along, teetering, correcting his balance and sometimes almost overdoing it. But it all comes out all right. Mother sees to that."

Safe trips over a high thin wire and over slender pliant boughs are, of course, much more difficult for juveniles to learn than how to scamper harmlessly about a thick tree trunk. Yet, like it or not,

30

they master the technique under the mother's patient—and sometimes impatient—tutelage. Within a few weeks, they have learned the trick and thereafter show no fear.

City and suburban squirrels necessarily permit biologists to judge much more accurately the extent of an individual's home range than do forest animals. In the forest any finding seems close to speculation. Estimates of ranges there vary widely, especially as regards the squirrel populations that existed in colonial times. The spread runs from one to fifty acres per individual. Squirrels in city and suburbs, lacking a forest in which to disappear, permit at least a rough count of numbers, indicating the range for each individual. In a New Haven, Connecticut, park, for example, twenty animals were found to live in two acres, or ten to an acre. In Central Park, the figure, at least at some points, was even higher. Van Gelder, as mentioned earlier, found thirty living within the acre and a half of his study. One of the more accurate conclusions about the range of suburban squirrels comes from Dr. Flyger's research on the outskirts of Washington, D.C. Feeding boxes placed near his home overlooking a heavily wooded, stream-filled ravine have attracted more than one hundred squirrels from the extensive sylvan territory nearby. By harmlessly trapping, marking, and studying them, he has determined a normal home range of about an acre and a half for each, in a habitat that, to a degree, approximates the forest.

A pecking order exists among squirrels, less rigidly, perhaps, in the forest than in the more crowded conditions of city and suburb. The hierarchy in any neighborhood is characteristically headed by a large old male. He is Number One, the Chairman of the Board. At feeding spots and in mating situations, Number Two defers to him, and so on down the line. Males dominate females (except in family situations), and adults dominate juveniles. The value of hierarchy as a survival technique is clear. It limits aggressive behavior, thus saving for the species time and energy that can be better put to life-sustaining activities.

To provide for winter needs, squirrels bury nuts. The number 31 put underground annually must be astronomical. City squirrels are as assiduous at this task as their forest brethren. A long-time observer of park squirrels, the naturalist Seton, reported on the ritual in his *Lives of Game Animals* as follows:

"His procedure is always the same. He receives the nut in his teeth, then takes it in both paws, puts it back in his mouth, turns it around, licks it with his tongue, then goes off a few bounds, and, with forepaws, digs a hole in some open place, making it about three inches deep. Holding the nut in his teeth, he rams it down point first into the hole; with his snout, he roots the earth back into place, tamps it down a little with his paws and his snout, replaces the leaves, combs up the grass with both paws, and goes off. If another squirrel comes near it at once, the owner of the cache drives him away."

Squirrels are not the only potential nut thieves repelled. Seton goes on to disclose that when a man started to dig up a newly buried nut in a park in Harrisburg, Pennsylvania, he was rushed by the animal that knocked his hand away. After fifteen minutes he tried again and there was no such reaction. The squirrel seemed to have forgotten the nut, or its sense of ownership had dimmed. Seton has related that he repeatedly watched park squirrels "bury ten out of thirteen peanuts within an hour, each in a separate hole." They did this, under his observation, every fine morning during the three months of the nut season—from mid-September to mid-December—and he calculated that in those months each eastern gray probably buried several thousand nuts, perhaps as many as ten thousand. When the wide range of the gray and other squirrel species is considered, the size of the annual trove of subterranean nuts is mind-boggling.

Not all researchers agree with Seton's description of the nut-burying act. Evidently squirrels, like human beings, vary considerably. Other observers note that they have seen burials at only half Seton's depth; still others have seen much deeper burials. Furthermore, some squirrels can hardly be said to bury at all. They merely shove a few leaves over the nut and walk away, acting all the while as though they had done a good job.

In winter, squirrels find and excavate the buried nuts by sense of smell, sometimes going down through two feet of snow to do so. I have seen one in Central Park on a mild day after a snowfall go through almost that depth to bring up a nut. The animals forage actively throughout the cold season, the only exceptions being very stormy or exceptionally frigid days. Then they remain in their shelters curled in a ball, the luxuriant tail wrapped about them like a coverlet, helping to keep the body temperature up. If there is more than one squirrel in the nest or den, then so much the cozier.

Another diet staple at this time, when food is in short supply, is twigs. These are thoroughly chewed and ingested. The animals in trees or on the ground seem especially active during drizzly days. As they sit or run along the branches, the tail is held like an umbrella over the head. To clear it of water drops, only a quick flick is needed, and it is again ready to serve as protection. Muscles in the tail permit the hair to lie completely flat or to stand entirely erect, according to its owner's fancy. The hairs of the tail are the last to go during molts, which occur in the spring and fall.

Though most gray squirrels, as the name implies, are exactly that color, some gray squirrels are totally black and some gray squirrels are pure white. These variants, part of a phenomenon shared by many species of animals, are known respectively as melanistic and albinistic squirrels. However, all are true gray squirrels. Anatomically they are the same. I have run across the black kind in Central Park. In the borough of The Bronx, farther north in New York City, they are not at all uncommon. The farther north one goes in the range, the more black squirrels there are. In fact, in the range's extreme north, which is the southern portion of eastern Canada, the melanistic squirrels often outnumber the normally colored grays.

In Central Park I was never able to see nor, despite faithful inquiry, find any record of albinistic squirrels there. My original article reported this. However, later I heard to the contrary from a woman correspondent; she gave me data on a specimen she had found there. In general, the albinistic squirrel is rarer than the black. Still, when a concentration of the former's genes occurs in a locality, an albino population can result. A number of albinos have been reported from Trenton, New Jersey, and more from Greenwood, South Carolina. There their living space has been estimated at about one hundred acres. The largest colony is in Olney, Illinois, in the southern part of the state. According to local legend, its origin stems from the desire of an Olney saloonkeeper in the 1890s for publicity. He somehow acquired a pair of albino squirrels that he kept in the window of his establishment. Their descendants now number several hundred. Over these, the town exerts a sort of parental responsibility. A motorist, for example, who strikes one is subject to a fine of twenty-five dollars. I have no information on how often this penalty has been invoked.

The handsome gray squirrel coats one sees on city streets are not the product of our own grays. At better stores, one of these garments, styled as a full-length coat, would cost twenty-five hundred dollars or more. It would be stitched from the skins of a species of gray squirrel indigenous to Russia. Unlike ours, the species has prettily tufted ears. Unlike ours, too, their fur, especially on the specimens from Siberia, is very dense. The chill of the climate there makes it so. Furriers describe the best of these skins as lustrous, fluffy, and steely blue gray with long thick ground hairs and slightly longer guard hairs. Squirrel-skin coats are not as tough and heavy as their wearers would like: The fur is called lightweight with fair to poor wearing qualities.

City squirrels, unsurprisingly, have given biologists their best idea of the species' swiftness. (Imagine the problems inherent in all-out pursuit of a woods squirrel by a scientist burdened with a device for measuring speed). Before giving figures on squirrel velocity, however, some facts first about their methods of locomotion. When the squirrel uses its legs alternately, it carries its tail, an important adjunct to all its movements, aloft in a restrained arch. More often, it travels in hops. Then front and hind legs work together, each pair functioning as a unit, the muscular back ones supplying the principal power. Normal hops are twelve inches. These increase to twenty-four inches when the squirrel is in low gear, and to three or four feet at ordinary high speed. When the animal is being closely pursued, the bounds can cover six feet at a time.

As for maximum straightaway speed, figures vary, but none are very fast. Were a direct course to be followed, a man could easily outrun a squirrel. A top sprinter, for instance, goes almost thirty miles an hour. For a short distance after the start, he can outdistance a racehorse. Squirrels, however, don't need straight-line speed to survive. They dodge superlatively, deftly using the tail as a counter-balance, whipping it this way and that to change their center of gravity. Their mastery of this tactic enables them to evade virtually any animal enemy that might wish to attack them on the ground. Trying to discover just how fast a squirrel could run, Seton pursued one down his driveway in an automobile. When the speedometer reached twelve miles an hour, Seton decided that the bounding animal could go no faster. Another authority gives ten miles an hour "if startled" as the top speed. A third, chasing one on foot with a stopwatch, recorded just under twelve miles an hour. Dr. F. S. Barkalow reports the work of two biologists at Cornell University who tested the speed of fifteen species of small mammals, all of which by various devices were made to run a straight line. The gray squirrel turned out to be the fastest, besting such competitors as the opossum, chipmunk, and red squirrel. The fastest of several grays ran at seventeen miles an hour. Squirrels, like people, apparently have a rather wide range of performance.

Far more spectacular than any progress on the ground are the acrobatics squirrels perform in trees. A squirrel can descend a tree practically as fast as it can ascend one. With one bound it can reach four feet up on a trunk. But its most stunning achievements are leaps from tree to tree. Watchers have often seen nearly incredible examples. One authority states that springy branches allow the tree-borne squirrel to increase its leaps substantially beyond the maximum five or six feet attained on the ground. Reports of as much as thirty-foot jumps have been verified. But the points of arrival in such giant passages—startling to watch—are always some distance lower than the takeoff. The squirrel, a projectilelike object in such a situation, is assured of safe landing during the latter stages of the flight by skillful use of the tail, which acts as an aerial rudder. These leaps are sometimes part of an effort to escape an enemy. During such dangers, the squirrel may change its mind, dive down twenty feet into the bushes and go through them like a shot. Or plummet on all fours to the ground and then make for the nearest tree. All authorities agree, however, that the gray in peril never seeks safety underground, as a beleaguered red squirrel may.

Animal literature abounds in accounts of dogs and cats that, often with great difficulty, have found their way home. One of the more unusual of these tales concerns a collie dog. Sent in the fall of one year from its mistress in Fort Scott, Kansas, to accompany her nephews to Albuquerque, New Mexico, the dog, obviously unhappy in its new surroundings, disappeared. A diligent search by the boys failed to find it. Eight months later, scarred, thin, and exhausted, it crawled through the summer-opened doorway of its Kansas home to drop at the feet of its mistress. On another occasion, a cat belonging to a couple I knew was AWOL when it came time for its owners to leave their vacation home, a hundred and fifty miles from their permanent residence. A hunt high and low and much calling failed to bring puss to light. Perforce the master and mistress left. Two months later, the cat rejoined its owners at home, quietly taking possession of a favorite corner of the sofa.

A squirrel has done this sort of thing, too. In Milwaukee, Wisconsin, a two-week-old orphaned gray fell from its nest and was adopted by a man and his wife. After a year had passed, the nearly full-grown squirrel stayed both in the house and outdoors, as suited its fancy. In time, it became friendly with passersby, who convinced the couple that the pet should be sent to the Humane Society. Accordingly, it was put in a cage and taken seven miles across town to society headquarters. Two weeks later, having negotiated an escape from the society and also traversed urban roofs, backyards, streets, and sidewalks, it presented itself at the back door of its old home, whose owners reported "it begged for food and water." The incident illustrates the initiative, ingenuity, courage, and persistence of a determined squirrel (as well as a power whose basis we do not yet understand, the mysterious homing instinct present in some animals).

A squirrel's life expectancy is unpredictable—at least as far as any individual is concerned. The majority of young squirrels, either of forest or city, probably don't survive their first year, a fate that seems to be that of most young wild things. But let a gray squirrel reach adulthood and it has been described as the master of any situation it is apt to encounter. Once adulthood is attained, a squirrel's life expectancy, most authorities feel, is from six to eight years. But, of course, there are examples of greater longevity. A number of records of both pet and wild squirrels reaching their teens exist. The longest-lived squirrel whose history I have come across, a pet, succumbed at twenty years of age.

3. EARLY TIMES

When the white man started colonization of our country, the land-scape differed markedly from today's. Behind the Atlantic seaboard, along which the pioneers hunkered down in a few tiny settlements, lay a stupendous forest peopled with countless squirrels. So tall and thick were the trees that, below their branches, twilight reigned all day. Of this time, a historian has said that a squirrel could travel from the Atlantic Ocean to the Mississippi River without once touching the ground. Most of the trees in this enormous, unbroken stretch of woodland were of the deciduous type, the preferred habitat of the gray squirrel. In all, the dense forest was made up of several hundred tree varieties. But even within the conifer-abundant north and south ends of this primeval sylva, enough hardwood species existed to support a population of grays. The major deciduous types, growing together in groups, according to the environment, were: beech-birch-maple; oak-hickory; oak-chestnut-yellow poplar; oak alone; and river-bottom hardwoods. All groups furnished ample food in the form of mast and acorns, foliage, buds, and flowers; and, 39 in the expansive sweep of the leafy interior, the natural cycle of decay was always at work, providing a plentiful supply of dens.

From this timbery stronghold, the squirrels soon made their presence known to the colonists. Of all the native Americans the newcomers met, the squirrels were far and away the most numerous. They descended in hordes on the little corn patches. Adding insult to injury, they ate (as they do today) only the germ part of the kernels, strewing the ground with the starchy pulp. They enjoyed among the settlers, almost from the first, a repugnant reputation. In time, resolute extermination campaigns against them were conducted. One, begun in 1749 by outraged officials in the colony of Pennsylvania, placed a bounty of three pence on each scalp. Six hundred and forty thousand squirrels were destroyed that year; the cost to the colonial treasury was eight thousand pounds sterling. A hundred years later, with anti-squirrel feeling still running high, two parties, each of six Kentuckians, came back after a week's hunt with almost ten thousand dead squirrels. And, about this same time, community shoots organized in western New York often accounted for as many as two thousand animals in a day. In the country's youth, all this seemed of no matter; squirrels were everywhere.

In those days, the species was known as a migrating animal. Often it was seen in vast numbers, usually in the fall of the year, moving through the woods, across cleared land and farms in a lemminglike action, over anything that was in its way, including mountains and bodies of water. The occurrence puzzled our ancestors. The participants seemed fat and healthy. Why should they travel? And the eruptions were erratic and unpredictable. But damaging. Very damaging. All cultivated areas in their path were devastated.

A description of these treks has been left by Dr. John Bachman, a naturalist and collaborator of Audubon, the famous ornithologist. Bachman had this to say about the furry tourists:

"The farmers in the western wilds regard them with sensations that may be compared to the anxious apprehensions of the Eastern nations at the flight of the devouring locust. At such periods, which usually occur in autumn, the Squirrels congregate in different districts of the far Northwest; and in irregular troops, bend their way instinctively in an eastern direction. Mountains, cleared fields, the narrow bays of some of our lakes, or our broad rivers, present no unconquerable impediments. Onward they come, devouring on the way everything that is suited to their taste, laying waste the corn and wheatfields of the farmer; and as their numbers are thinned by the gun, the Dog, and the club, others fall in and fill up the ranks, till they occasion infinite mischief, and call forth more than empty threats of vengeance.

"Ordinarily averse to entering the water, they now take to it boldly, and, though swimming with difficulty, manage to cross broad rivers, like the Niagara and Ohio, though many are drowned in the attempt. . . .

"Sometimes, when on these migrations, especially after crossing

rivers, the Squirrels become so fatigued as to be easily captured, and thousands are then killed by boys, armed merely with sticks and stones. I learned from Dr. John A. Kennicott that, during one of these migrations, innumerable Squirrels swam across the river Niagara and landed near Buffalo, New York, in such a state of exhaustion that the boys caught them in their hands, or knocked them from the fences and bushes with poles.

"They swam the Hudson in various places between Waterford and Saratoga; those which we observed crossing the river, were swimming deep and awkwardly, their bodies and tails wholly submerged; several that had been drowned were carried downwards by the stream, and those which were so fortunate as to reach the opposite bank, were so wet and fatigued, that the boys stationed there with clubs found no difficulty in securing them alive, or in killing them. Their migrations on that occasion did not, so far as we could learn, extend further eastward than the mountains of Vermont; many remained in the county of Rensselaer, and it was remarked that for several years afterwards Squirrels were far more numerous there than before. It is doubtful whether any ever return to the West, as finding forests and food suited to their taste and habits, they take up their permanent residence in their newly explored country, where they remain and propagate their species, until they are gradually thinned off by the increase of inhabitants, new clearings, and the dexterity of sportsmen around them.

"After one of these grand migrations, very few of the species are found in the localities from which they have moved, and these, as if alarmed at the unusual solitude, are silent and shy. They rapidly increase in numbers, however, and in a few years are as abundant as before."

Despite Bachman's emphasis on movements from west to east, the migrations on various occasions have been witnessed heading to all points of the compass. In 1842, for instance, an enormous migration went out of Wisconsin to the southwest, and lasted four weeks. According to rough data compiled at the time, it was an army one hundred and thirty miles wide and one hundred and fifty miles long. From a road, where vision was limited to a few yards on either side, an observer counted fourteen hundred animals within two miles. A modern naturalist has estimated that the assemblage must have contained half a billion squirrels.

Testimony on the amount and success of squirrel aquatic activity is mixed. While Bachman indicates they are averse to enter water except on migration, other authorities say they take to it whenever they feel so inclined. Nor do they lose their wits there. The observer who tells this tale states that a lone squirrel swimming in a lake saw a canoe. Promptly it made toward it. The canoeist put out his paddle, the squirrel climbed on it, and was taken aboard. During the voyage, it sat quietly in the bow. When the canoe beached, off it jumped and hopped briskly into the woods, a more well-behaved passenger being hard to imagine. Many watchers have described the squirrel not as an inept, but as a good swimmer. It uses a strong, steady dog paddle with which it can easily cover two miles in calm water. Under such conditions, witnesses say, it holds it head and rump high out of the water. The mouth and nostrils are then clear, and the ears laid flat. Sometimes the tail is held behind it in the air, at others it is maintained just over the surface. Rough water cuts its speed. Then the tail, with its hair raised, may be immersed and hold some air. To avoid a threatened blow, a squirrel will dive. But it is a shallow effort of about eighteen inches, and of short duration. A report from Russia has squirrels swimming in the saltwater of the Gulf of Bothnia, part of the Baltic Sea, which separates Russia from Sweden. Doubtless these are the same squirrels as those used by our furriers for squirrel coats. In our country, I have run across no records of grays swimming in saltwater.

In considering the squirrel's history in early times, one can regress to *very* early times—to, in fact, the middle Oligocene period thirty million years ago, when there is a fossil record in North America of a squirrellike forebear. By the early Miocene, ten million years later, the squirrel stock had separated into genera, and the 43 animal we're interested in was very much like today's, about the same size as now, an arboreal creature with a tail. Many of the trees where it gamboled bore nuts. And on the landscape below it could see the early horses, primitive camels, and dog-toothed carnivores. You may be sure it kept a sharp eye on the last. But to infix all the fine points of the species, it probably took at least twenty-five million years from its non-generic ancestor for our gray to become the carefree frisker of our parks and woods.

Taxonomically the squirrel is a rodent, a member of the world's most numerous order of mammals, embracing more than half the kinds of living mammals and containing over a thousand rodent species, of which the largest is the capybara of South America, and the smallest is the mouse. All are characterized by sharp incisor teeth with which they gnaw. The gray squirrel's taxonomic pedigree is as follows:

Class:	Mammalia
Order:	Rodentia
Family:	Sciuridae
Genus:	Sciurus
Species:	Sciurus carolinensis

The gray squirrel was first described scientifically from a specimen taken in the Carolina region. The final word in the species name refers to this location. Just where in the Carolina region it was taken I have not been able to discover. In fact, the whole naming process seems a bit cloudy. A scientist called Gmelin is credited as the namer. The Gmelins were a scientifically prominent German family of the eighteenth century and later, and the namer seems to have been Johan Friedrich Gmelin. As far as I have been able to learn, he was never in this country. Therefore the squirrel must have been described from a specimen shipped to him in Europe, perhaps in the form of skeleton and skin. The animal first appears in scientific literature in the thirteenth edition of Linnaeus's *Systema Natura*, published in 1788, of which Gmelin was the editor.

The squirrel's common name, on the other hand, goes back far into recorded history. It began with the ancient Greeks. Aristotle used the word. It was *skiouros*, formed of the roots *skia*, or shade, and *oura*, tail, meaning "he who sits in the shadow of his tail." It later went into formal Latin as *scurius*. Some centuries afterward the Old French noun *esquirel* was created from the diminutive of Vulgar Latin's *scurellus*, from *scurius*. From this came our present word, squirrel.

The squirrel throughout its history was, of course, threatened by predators. One of the more interesting was the red-tailed hawk, an enterprising and sometimes—but not always—successful squirrel hunter. When a single hawk approached, the squirrel would circle the trunk of a tree so rapidly and deftly that the bird was made to look foolish. But when a pair of hawks arrived as they often did—seemingly with appreciation of the virtue of the tactic—it was a different story. Then, unless the squirrel could dive into its den, it had a problem. The hawks would course rapidly from opposite sides of the trunk to which the squirrel clung. The distracted animal, keeping an eye on the closer hawk, soon lost track of the other, whose talons would shortly find its back.

Rarer foes were the marten and fisher, tree-climbing weasels that are lightning fast. Although the marten is swift, the fisher, the larger of the pair, is even swifter. It is said that if anything could go faster in a tree than a fisher, it would have to fly. The squirrel, for all its arboreal speed and grace, is no match for either. Its only hope is to find a hollow whose small opening prevents the predator's entry. Fortunately for the gray, both species were relatively uncommon and restricted in range, limits that are even more pronounced today.

By the end of the Civil War in 1865, the gray squirrel's homeland had undergone considerable change. Where once the uninterrupted forest had stood, clearings, pastures, farms, villages, towns, 45 and even cities had taken over part of the land. In the period of peace that followed the conflict, the process continued apace. As the decades slipped by, the effect on the squirrels became serious. In fact, by 1900, some biologists feared the eastern grays' days were numbered; the species, they believed, was marked for extinction.

Oddly enough, while this was going on in the wild, the number of squirrels in Central Park reached their greatest abundance. The park at this time was notably hospitable toward them. At the start of this century, the park had been open for forty years. It was then far, far closer to being the idyllic recreational spot that its gifted designers, Frederick Law Olmsted and Calvert Vaux, had in mind for it than it is today. It was much wilder then, and far fewer visitors trudged through it than the more than twelve million who annually frequent it at present. Furthermore, the users then were much more careful of the environment. In the remoter precincts of the park, a number of little-used sections existed. Wandering into one, a pedestrian might feel that a real part of nature was dozing nearby. For example, a large, tree-shaded rock (since removed to make an entrance for automobiles at 106th Street and Central Park West) contained numerous crevices. In them, the late, well-known herpetologist, Raymond L. Ditmars, found scores of brown and garter snakes. The crevices served as hibernation dens for the creatures, which in mild weather roamed the park at will. The muskrat was also present then. So were various species of the shyer wildfowl, inhabiting the lakes and ponds. Trees and all other living things benefited greatly from the absence of the automobile and its fumes.

The squirrels of this period, descended from native stock on the original park site, thrived. Then, as now, they were supported by the handouts of visitors. As a result, they increased to such an extent that a thinning of their ranks became necessary. In one week during 1901, the squirrel population, then estimated to number more than a thousand, was reduced by three hundred. Park attendants shot them. They were easy to bag, having no fear of human beings, whom they had come to regard over the years as their friends.

46

Hunting squirrels in the wild is another matter. Bringing one down is usually regarded as one of the hunter's more difficult tasks because the squirrel, if it cannot reach the safety of a hollow, flattens itself on top of a lofty branch until it seems barely more than a wisp of gray lichen. In the nation's early days, squirrels, as has been mentioned, were everywhere in the wilderness. They were, of course, just as canny then and hard to shoot. But the pioneers of the time, needing them for the pot, became good enough with their long rifles to knock squirrels off the limbs in quantity.

An admiring minor note appeared during the country's bicentennial celebration four years ago to emphasize the effect this marksmanship had on our history. The account stated:

"A hero of the American Revolution is out on a limb, likely to be overlooked for the country's 200th birthday. He didn't fire the shot heard round the world. But in his way he taught the colonists how to shoot straighter than men from any other land—straight enough, in a twanging ballad of the hills, to 'knock a squirrel's eye out at 90 feet.' Old Grayback or Silvertail, as some still call him, is in fact the gray squirrel, *Sciurus carolinensis*. In the skirmishes of the Revolution, backwoodsmen with their long-barreled Kentucky squirrel rifles used to say that it took a redcoat his weight in lead to hit and kill an American, but Yankee bullets, about ninety to the pound, found their marks every time. British soldiers frequently discovered that such point-blank bragging was backed up by deadeye marksmanship, learned in a world where the day's food was often rifle-won. The seemingly awkward long squirrel rifle astonished new arrivals from Europe, but its accuracy is impressive even today."

It was nowhere more so than at the Battle of New Orleans during the War of 1812. The hot-tempered Andrew Jackson was the American commander. The British with their large navy moved to attack the virtually defenseless city from the sea, aided by a large force of infantry in troop transports. The energetic Jackson threw up defenses, beat back the first British assault, and called vociferously for reinforcements. These—from Kentucky and Tennessee, crack shots to a man—were granted, bringing his force to some five thousand strong. At dawn on January 8, 1815, the main force of the British, in strength twice that of Jackson's, launched its grand assault against the Americans, who were holed up behind a strong defense line. Before they withdrew, the attackers, under the deadly American fire, were cut down in droves. More than two thousand men, including the top British generals, were lost against American casualties of twelve killed. It was the only major land battle won by our side during the war, a magnificent victory, unquestionably to be credited to the squirrels.

Later, during the Civil War, fear of the same deadly rifle fire turned back a Confederate threat to invade the state of Ohio when fifty thousand squirrel hunters volunteered for home defense.

The reason our forefathers hunted the squirrel was its tasty meat. Subsisting mainly on acorns and nuts, a woods squirrel's flesh has a pleasant, satisfying flavor. It was, I said in the original magazine article, an essential ingredient in a colonial delicacy, Brunswick stew, now almost forgotten. This provoked within weeks a spirited and informative rejoinder from that cradle of traditionalism and that prop of colonial ideals, the Old Southland. A gentleman columnist of *The News Leader* of Richmond, Virginia, wrote in part as follows:

"The other month *The New Yorker* magazine undertook a study of squirrels and, covering the subject thoroughly observed that once they were an ingredient in an exotic, now almost forgotten, Southern dish, Brunswick stew.

"Almost forgotten?

"At this very moment, somewhere in central Virginia, a stewmaster is stirring a smoke-wreathed iron pot suspended from a tripod or set above the fire on cinder blocks.

"Many a political career, Sunday School hall, or volunteer firehouse has been based on Brunswick stew. The dish was discovered, Virginians assert, in Brunswick County, Va. Indeed, it is that county's proudest boast, next to being the birthplace of Gov. Albertis Harrison.

"A county of the same name in North Carolina and an attorney of Brunswick, Ga., also claim to have originated the stew. The Georgians went so far as to propose a monument, but fell apart over whether to erect it in the shape of the founder of the dish. [By which, I take it, is meant the squirrel itself.]

"The stew is the subject of much debate. Even in Brunswick County, Va., there is disagreement over whether the first pot was brewed on the banks of the Meherrin River or on the Nottoway.

"A history of Brunswick County, 'Brunswick's Story,' by Edith Rethbun Bell and William Lightfoot Heartwell, Jr., sifted the accounts and decided the stew was first cooked in Red Oak District on the banks of the Nottoway. The historians credit 'Uncle Jimmy' Matthews, 'a retainer of Dr. Creed Haskins who lived at Mount Donum on the Nottoway River,' with being the creator.

"Their account rules out the myth that a party of hunters from Powhatan County left one of their number in camp to prepare the evening meal and he, being lazy, simply threw everything into a pot and let 'er stew. The others, when they returned, were indignant until one of them, sampling the fare, said, 'Hey, this ain't half bad.'

"The first stew, the two historians say, was largely squirrel, plus onions, bits of bacon, butter, and crumbled stale bread for thickening. . . . Chicken has long since supplanted squirrel in the pot.

"The height of the Brunswick stew season coincides with the arrival of fresh vegetables in late summer or early fall. The stewmaster starts his fire before 5 A.M. and adds the meat, butterbeans, corn, tomatoes, potatoes, carrots, and whatnot at exact intervals until, after seven or eight hours, it is all cooked down. . . . In Dinwiddie County, Lunsford Butterworth has a castiron pot that holds 125 gallons. 'It takes four good people to lift it,' he observed. Some people, he noted, add bread, cracker crumbs, or oatmeal for thickening, but he relies on the pure ingredients, including creamery butter."

Although the gentleman columnist states (and, in fact, to my satisfaction proves) that Brunswick stew is indeed not forgotten, he seems to say that the original essential ingredient, squirrel meat, is no longer used. Modern cookbooks apparently agree, at least those I have found that list the dish. They, too, specify chicken. The reason for this lamentable replacement, those knowledgeable in such matters tell me, is that squirrels are no longer handy to bag, too difficult to skin once bagged, and too spare of meat to be worth the trouble of capture and preparation when easier, if less flavorsome, meat is available. Such acquiescence to convenience, widely practiced today, is called progress. In light of the new knowledge from Richmond, Virginia, I feel that what I should have said is that the squirrel was originally the essential ingredient in a colonial delicacy known as Brunswick stew, but its use in that dish is now almost forgotten.

From 1900 to 1915, and perhaps for a decade or so before that, a dominant figure in the movement to restore our forests was Gifford Pinchot, eventually the founder of the Yale School of Forestry, who went on to become the governor of Pennsylvania. With the rehabilitation of our woodlands, the decline of the gray squirrel came to an end. It began instead to increase in its old territories and thereafter spread to those parts of suburbia and other haunts of man where it was not already present. In general, in the larger city parks, it had been unaffected by what had been going on in the woods and its numbers in the parks had remained more or less steady. However, with the increasing wild population, the old migratory outbursts resumed. Not at once. And not as stupendous as formerly. But large enough.

In the mid-thirties, there were several mass movements westward from New England to New York. Thousands of squirrels were seen swimming the Connecticut River between Hartford and Essex. At the Hudson, they crossed, where possible, by bridge and ferryboat; otherwise, they took to the water. Many other migrations succeeded these. The largest one in recent times took place in the fall of 1968—in the month of September, to be exact, the month that historically had been favored for this activity. Certainly hundreds of thousands, and perhaps the twenty millions that were given by one estimate, were on the move. Most eastern states from Georgia to Vermont were affected. Squirrels appeared on highways, lawns, golf courses, in natural bodies of water and in man-made ones such as swimming pools and reservoirs, and in other spots where ordinarily they were at least uncommon, if not lacking altogether. The number of dead squirrels on highways was great. One hundred were found on a twenty-seven-mile stretch near Asheville, North Carolina; 223 on a 205-mile trip taken by a zoologist from Pennsylvania to New York. The wanderers seemed confused, especially on the roads. As cars approached, they were seen to jump into the air, zigzag back and forth, and otherwise behave erratically. One biologist who examined corpses found the skin on the foot pads unusually thin, probably, he thought, from the great distances traveled, and surmised that the animals on the road could feel the vibrations of the oncoming automobiles, which caused them to panic. Another discounted this, saying that wild squirrels, unlike their city relatives, were simply unfamiliar with the motor car, and that this led to their strange behavior.

Four teams of scientists from the Universities of Georgia, Maryland, and Missouri and from the Smithsonian Institution in Washington, D.C., sallied forth to monitor the event. The Smithsonian at this time had just founded the Center for the Study of Short-Lived Phenomena, a unit whose function was to note meteorite falls, insect infestations, volcanic eruptions, pollution accidents, and other events of short duration that occur on our planet, so that scientists, alerted by a network of Center informants, could get to the site and study the phenomenon before it passed.

The objective of the scientific teams was to scrutinize and ponder the acts of the squirrels, and to collect specimens. These last greatly contributed to the mystery of the movement, just as had been the case in earlier times. The migrants seemed fat. And the areas they left had good food supplies. Nor did the scholars subscribe to theories that psychological stress or parasites had caused the out-

51

break. Since many of the travelers were young, the best supposition was that migrations provided a convenient population dispersal maneuver.

The scientist who made the closest study of the movement was a member of the University of Maryland team, Dr. Vagn Flyger. For most of his life he had been interested in squirrels, and for many years of his professional career he had concentrated his research on them. He turned his report in to the Center for the Study of Short-Lived Phenomena. One of its conclusions was that to learn more about the causes for squirrel migrations observers, wherever they might be, should promptly notify the Center so that scientists could gather to investigate. On the basis of Flyger's, and other, data, the Center estimated that the 1968 migration contained twenty million squirrels. A few years after the Center was founded, the normally saturnine Soviet Academy of Sciences was heard to comment that "some say this is the greatest scientific information service" yet devised. The first report contained in the files of this greatest scientific information service is Flyger's on the 1968 squirrel migration. (The Center is now disassociated from the Smithsonian and has its headquarters in Cambridge, Massachusetts.)

An event which may or may not be in the Center's annals, but which very well could be (and perhaps should be) is the great acorn shortage in the Northeast in 1978. Not only did this deficiency have an adverse effect on squirrels but it worked a hardship, too, on a sector of our economy not known by most of our citizens to exist—the acorn brokers. Yes, the acorn brokers. These are not woods squirrels that gather and hoard acorns, passing them out for favors to other squirrels, but business firms, at least two of which have come to my attention in the Northeast. These concerns have acorns collected by contract in the forests. Squirrels, of course, collect them there, too. The acorns, when they are found, are sold by the pound—ninety-six red oak acorns on the average to the pound, for example. The broker's customers are men who sell trees. Often two or three nurserymen are involved before the trees are ultimately set out on a lawn or elsewhere, eventually perhaps to provide food for the squirrels. In this sequence, there may be a grower who plants the acorn and sells the one-year tree, a mere whip, to another. The second may be one who nurses the stripling till branches develop. Then a third may take over to put some heft on the tree before it leaves for its final destination.

But in 1978 my two acorn brokers had very little trade. That year the two trees that are the main producers of their acorns had bad years, the white oak suffering from a late, wet spring, and the red oak, a heavy producer in alternate years, being in a light year. One broker in White Plains, New York, whom I spoke with said all the meager supply that his gatherers had been able to separate from the squirrels had been sold. At this point in time, the unobtrusive acorn broker and his stealthy, forest-plodding minions may be lumped together as the squirrel's least recognized adversaries.

4. GREAT BRITAIN

Great Britain has a large population of American gray squirrels, which have been established there for at least one hundred years. Nobody knows just where or when the successful introduction was made, but it is possible that the first were brought into the kingdom by Benjamin Franklin. One of my Harvard correspondents, who called this to my attention, labeled Franklin "a squirrel person," meaning that he was partial to, or distinctly interested in, squirrels. In light of Franklin's history, I feel that this is not a misnomer.

One of the things that makes Franklin notable—apart, of course, from his interest in squirrels—is his vigor and success as a diplomat even when he grew old. Soon after he turned fifty, he went to London for a five-year stay as a representative of the colony of Pennsylvania in a long drawn-out dispute with the Crown about lands claimed by the Penn family. He negotiated a partial compromise and, as a good diplomat should, made many friends. They were attracted, bemused, and often admiring of Franklin, who certainly was a character in the larger sense of the word. After a two-year stay back in America, he returned to Great Britain in 1764 on the same matter. Shortly thereafter he was drawn into the hullabaloo raised by passage of the Stamp Act. Before long he became the London representative of several other colonies, for which he tried to press the American side of the ever-widening argument about taxation.

Nor was he above using squirrels as a diplomatic lever. One of his friends was the Anglican bishop Jonathan Shipley, a leader in Britain of the pro-American cause. Franklin spent time with him as a guest in his country place at Twyford, in Hampshire, and at his town house in London. In 1771, Franklin had his wife in Philadelphia ship a squirrel named Mungo as a pet to the bishop's young daughter, Georgiana, who, understandably, was delighted with it. Mungo the squirrel was an extremely gentle and well-behaved Philadelphian, admirably reflecting the Quakerism of his place of birth. Another squirrel from the same shipment went to the children of the first Earl Spencer and his wife.

Franklin kept an alert custodial eye upon his gifts. In August 1772, seven months after the newcomers had arrived, he wrote his wife that "The squirrels still live and are great favourites in the Bishop's and Lady Spencer's families." However, shortly thereafter tragedy struck Mungo. In September of that same year the squirrel left the house at Twyford and wandered onto an adjacent heath where a man was walking a dog. The dog threatened Mungo which, knowing only kindness and trust from human beings, fled to the man and leaped on his shoulder. The man, naturally enough frightened by the action of this unfamiliar animal, shook him off and the dog killed him. Mungo was buried—with, one hopes, appropriate Anglican ceremonies—and Georgiana wrote Franklin requesting an epitaph for the funereal monument. In response, Franklin penned the following letter:

Dear Miss,

I lament with you most sincerely the unfortunate end of poor Mungo. Few Squirrels were better accomplished; for he had a good education, had travelled far, and seen much of the world. As he had the honor of being, for his virtues, your favourite, he should not go, like common skuggs, without an elegy or epitaph. [Skugg at the time was a common British expression for squirrel, much as puss is for cat. Today it is a countrified term, the spelling given in Webster's Unabridged being scug.] Let us give him one in the monumental style and measure, which, being neither prose nor verse, is perhaps the properest for grief; since to use common language would look as if we were not affected, and to make rhymes would seem trifling in sorrow.

EPITAPH

Alas! poor Mungo!
Happy wert thou, hadst thou known
Thy own felicity.
Remote from the fierce bald eagle,
Tyrant of thy native woods,
Thou hadst nought to fear from his piercing talons,
Nor from the murdering gun
Of the thoughtless sportsman.
Safe in thy wired castle,
GRIMALKIN could never annoy thee.
Daily wert thou fed with the choicest viands,
By the fair hand of an indulgent mistress;
But, discontented,
Thou wouldst have more freedom.

Too soon, alas! didst thou obtain it;
  And wandering,
Thou are fallen by the fangs of wanton, cruel RANGER!

  Learn hence,
Ye who blindly seek more liberty,
  Whether subjects, sons, squirrels or daughters,
  That apparent restraint may be real protection;
    Yielding peace and plenty
      With security.

You see, my dear Miss, how much more decent and proper this broken style is, than if we were to say, by way of epitaph,

  Here SKUGG
  Lies snug
  As a bug
  In a rug.

and yet, perhaps, there are people in the world of so little feeling as to think that this would be a good-enough epitaph for poor Mungo.

If you wish it, I shall procure another to succeed him; but perhaps you will now choose some other amusement.

Remember me affectionately to all the good family, and believe me ever,

Your affectionate friend,
B. Franklin

Georgiana did wish a replacement and Franklin shortly thereafter wrote his wife, Deborah, in Philadelphia to send one. There was some delay in the matter. Deborah wrote Franklin "I have had very bad luck with two squirrels. One was killed and another ran away although they were used to me. I have not had a cage as I don't know

58

where the man lives that makes them." However, in October of 1773 in that same letter, her last surviving one to Franklin, Deborah wrote that she was dispatching a squirrel to Miss Shipley aboard a merchantman under the command of Captain Awl, and that she hoped that with this one the recipient would have "better luck." Ultimately, for transatlantic voyages were long in those days, the squirrel reached Twyford in fine fettle. Two years later Franklin, sensing war was inevitable, left Great Britain and the donated skuggs for his

homeland. In May of 1779, when he was in his early seventies and the American colonies' representative to France, working with the skill and vigor of a man many years his junior to further our cause in the Revolutionary War, Georgiana, then twenty-three years old, wrote this to Franklin in Paris concerning her pet: "The American squirrel is still living and much caressed, poor fellow!; he has grown quite old and has lost his eyesight, but nevertheless preserves his spirits and wonted activity." A typical Yankee gray, one might say.

Although Franklin's squirrels might have been the first to set foot in Great Britain, presumably they are not responsible for the droves of grays that are there today. All apparently lacked a spouse, thus eliminating them from the charge of furthering the genocide of British squirrels, an accusation that often during this century has been leveled against the unwelcome arrivals.

The squirrel native to Great Britain is a red one, noticeably smaller and less powerful than our gray; in appearance, in fact, it is much like our own red squirrel although of a less pugnacious disposition. In early English history it, and supposedly no grays at all, inhabited most of the island wherever there were trees. Its preferred haunts, though, were evergreen groves. Seeds from the cones of conifers were what it liked best to eat.

Paleologically speaking, the English red squirrel is a relative newcomer to its homeland. No fossils are found there before the glacial period. It is thought to have arrived from Europe sometime after the most recent ice age and not long before the last land link between the island and the continent was broken, roughly seven thousand years ago.

About a half century after Franklin brought his ostensibly unfruitful grays to the country, a mysterious report of others surfaced in natural-history records. The animals were sighted in secluded country in Wales. One was shot in 1828. An equally mysterious, and what may be an even earlier, report came from the other side of the country. In East Kent a man who was born shortly after the middle of the last century, and who for many years had been a forest official, told a woman correspondent of an English magazine that gray squirrels were present around his home when he was a boy. He said his father and grandfather, too, had mentioned them and they were, in his opinion, unquestionably indigenous. A curious aftermath of this remark is that the correspondent, also from East Kent, said in her letter of fifty years ago that she, as well, had seen gray squirrels in that area and "I can only say that those I have seen there are much smaller than the ones to be found in Hyde Park." Fifty years

ago examples of *Sciurus carolinensis* were all over London's Hyde

Park, all of them much larger than the native reds. However, the woman said that the East Kent squirrels were smaller, leaving the door open for a race of native grays. By contrast, those seen in Wales were described as larger animals, much the size of the American ones. Both reports remain unexplained, and no subsequent substantiation of either has surfaced.

The first gray squirrels known to have produced offspring were brought into England in 1876, or shortly before. A Mr. Brocklehurst, of Cheshire, a county on the west-central seacoast of England, imported two pair and, after keeping them caged on his estate at Henbury Park for a while, released them into the woods on the property in 1876. They thrived. Their descendants were numerous before the arrival of other contingents loosed in the same county following the start of this century. Eight years later, in Nottingham County, some forty miles to the east, a pair were shot. Their origin is unaccounted for; others seen there, however, suggest an unrecorded implantation.

In 1889 the floodgates opened. Squirrel arrivals grew commonplace. A Mr. G. S. Page of New Jersey brought over more than a dozen. Five, set free in a park in Middlesex County, just outside London, failed to live, but nearly a dozen furnished to the Duke of Bedford, and given their liberty by him in Bedfordshire, a few miles north of Middlesex, had far better luck. They soon set about colonizing the woods and breeding. They did so well that eventually eight liberations in various parts of the country were made from this stock. Landowners wished to display the novelty in pens or cages on their estates, or in the woods around them; a few squirrels were acquired by zoological gardens. Many more introductions occurred in the ensuing decades. In the early 1890s, a Canadian resident of Scottish descent brought several to Scotland and freed them on the shores of an inlet named Lake Long on the west coast in Dumbartonshire, north of Glasgow, from where they soon spread to the adjacent county of Stirling. One of the more prominent batches about this time was some one hundred animals kept by an American in his private menagerie at Richmond outside London. Eventually he re- 61 leased them all and they migrated to the extensive grounds of nearby Richmond Park, where they set up housekeeping.

Virtually all the grays brought into Britain after 1876 found the scene to their liking, and in due course spread across the country. Of the nearly ninety thousand square miles contained in England, Scotland, and Wales, descendants of our gray squirrels are found in better than twenty thousand square miles, an extensive range when one considers the amount of land that is treeless and uninhabitable by them. They also now, again by importation, occupy a good deal of Ireland.

As their spread continued in the 1920s and 1930s, the attitude toward them in Great Britain changed. At first hailed for their attractive appearance and friendly ways, residents of the island began to find them increasingly annoying. The feeling of antipathy has continued uninterruptedly to the present day. Last year when I was in England, a Midlands man said to me, "I'll tell you what your squirrels are capable of. When no one was looking, one of them slipped down a tree and ate half the exhibits at my wife's church's open-air home produce show. *That's* what your squirrels are capable of." A common name for them today in Great Britain is tree rat. They are charged with raiding gardens and orchards. In the spring and summer several years ago, a total of two hundred and seventy were shot in the walled garden of a large house in Surrey in an effort to protect the strawberry beds. Even so, the disgruntled owner said the squirrels pilfered at least half the crop. They have also been accused of eating the eggs and chicks of song and game birds, and devastating plantations of sycamore trees by peeling the bark from limbs to get at the sugary sap. One British author has stated, "I know of more than one patriotic Englishman who has been embittered against the whole American nation on account of the presence of their squirrels in his garden." In 1937 the government took cognizance of this attitude. It became illegal to import grays, or even to keep one without an official license. The edicts, of course, seem not to have troubled the squirrels at all. In town and country, their numbers are large.

They gather in London's Regent's Park today in companies comparable to those in Central Park and brazenly cadge sweets and other handouts from visitors, being as cheeky panhandlers there as here.

While I would by no means put it past a gray squirrel in this country to slip down a tree, when people's backs were turned, and consume half the exhibits of an outdoor home produce show, I think there is a reason for the gray's omnivorous appetite overseas, which so surprises and outrages our British cousins. Primarily, the gray consumes nuts. British sylva is notably lacking in nut trees. Its bare score of native species (contrasted to our several hundred) contain only two common acorn producers compared to our upwards of fifty oak species. And hickories, the gray's favorite nut tree, are absent completely. Set down in such an environment, and able to colonize it in an extensive way, *Sciurus carolinensis*, to keep body and soul together, eats what it can. Since a gray squirrel can tolerate a varied menu, I suspect that every charge made against it might be true. My explanation (which is also an apology) certainly makes it no less of a pest. But the resentment of those across the Atlantic may be eased somewhat by knowing that it is not completely a malevolent, unprincipled fiend.

Above all else, the gray squirrel is condemned in Great Britain for the belief, tenaciously held by the residents, that it seeks to exterminate the native red, and that ultimately it will be successful in doing so. The conviction, in all likelihood, is false. History shows decided ups and downs in the red squirrel population. Long before Franklin brought his pets to Great Britain, deforestation of the evergreen stands in the Highlands of Scotland almost eliminated the red there. But in the late eighteenth century, when landowners began planting trees, the squirrels rebounded. Now some say they are a nuisance there. In England, they were so numerous around London in the early eighteenth century that the twenty-odd thousand that were annually shot for food for city residents were taken nearby without, apparently, causing any diminution of the animal's numbers. However, toward the end of the last century, when the grays 63 were being seriously introduced and, unchecked by natural enemies, were spreading rapidly, an epidemic hit the red squirrels and consequently their great decline was popularly attributed to the arrival of the grays.

Today things look better for the native breed. The two species will probably coexist successfully with, perhaps, some mild friction wherever their two different habitats border—the grays being in deciduous forests and the reds in their favored evergreen surroundings.

The record of American gray squirrels as pets in Great Britain, begun by Franklin, did not end with him. One of my correspondents, a lawyer, in Portland, Oregon, contributes the saga of a pair that entered the country shortly before the great influx of grays began.

Mr. Charles E. Wright wrote as follows:

"After reading the letter . . . regarding the emigration of gray squirrels to England, I thought you might be interested in this addendum.

"In 1875 my great-grandmother, Harriette Pares, who was making her first visit from England to this country was commissioned by a young cousin of hers to bring back to England a pair of gray squirrels. She did so and gave an account of the return voyage on the steamship Russia with the squirrels in their heavy cages being pitched onto the floor of the cabin in a heavy storm. She nevertheless landed safely in Liverpool with her charges, took them to various country houses where they were greatly admired, finally placing them in the hands of a guard on a train to London.

"The young cousin, Nina Paget, who was a neighbor of Beatrix Potter, then nine years old, loaned the squirrels to her and it is believed that one of them may have been the model for 'Squirrel Nutkin.' "

While Mr. Wright turned out to be incorrect about the Squirrel Nutkin reference, his mention of the grays serving as a Potter story model may have some substance, a matter that will be discussed later.

In response to my note of thanks, he kindly offered the pertinent text of his relative's letter for my use. In doing so, he noted that it was addressed to his grandmother from her mother and that he had edited it slightly. It perhaps deserves reproduction in full as illustrative of the impressions of an upper-class English lady while traveling here and abroad a century ago. The unexplained proper names in the letter are English friends or acquaintances of the writer except for Alice, another daughter. Punctuation remains as was.

Leicester, England
October 29, 1875

My dearest Emily:

I will now tell you about my journey. I hope Alice will consider this as much her letter as yours, and that you will at once send it on to her. She will remember perhaps that I was very "seedy" the day I left Milwaukee. Mr. Mather's friend was very kind and on reaching Chicago saw me into the omnibus and told me where to get my ticket. I was then feeling better, though very weary and as soon as I could I took possession of my "drawing room" and the sofa. At 8 o'clock I went to bed and as I had a tolerable night I felt rested and better in the morning. At Niagara I went to the Clifton House where I fell in with some pleasant sociable English people and where I spent two nights. I think the falls quite sublime and would not have missed them on any account. An English gentleman walked with me to the American side, taking me to every point of *interest*, but of course I did not go *under* the fall. The weather was lovely. On Thursday Mr. and Mrs. Carruthers and I travelled as far as Albany, they being on their way to England from New Zealand where he is a person of some influence. We went on by train to New York. We should have done better had we gone by boat, but as it was we saw the Hudson very well and admired it greatly. I even thought I should not object to live between New York and Albany. We travelled in a drawing room car, different to my "through drawing room" and holding about 15 people, each having an armchair which turned to any side you pleased. In a chair near me was a very gentlemanlike man who quite neglected his companion in order to give me information about the places we passed, much to the satisfaction of Mr. Carruthers who wanted to hear all he could. He assisted us to the station and recommended us to go to the Everett House in Union Square which is conducted on the European system and where we were very comfortable. I hoped the Carruthers would go by the Russia, that being their intention if possible, but they could not get the cabin they wanted and so eventually they took their passage by the Britannic which was to sail three days later than the Russia.

We became great friends and hope to meet in London where they stay three months and then return to New Zealand—a country Mr. C. tried to persuade me I should like.

On Saturday I sent a note to Mr. Rathbone who came posthaste and of course wanted me to go to the opera, to Tiffany's and various other places, but I told him I was too tired. He got me my squirrels and of course saw me on board, introducing me to the Captain and procuring me any amount of attention.

The weather was cold but very fine and so calm up to the 15th when we sailed into a terribly heavy sea, and not a passenger but was down. The sea was so high it washed over the upper deck, and not a breath of air could be admitted by port or skylight. We were in the Gulf Stream too and the heat was intolerable; you might have wrung my hair. Then the sea dashed through a skylight making no end of work for the stewards; one side of the ship (not mine) being flooded. Meanwhile I held on as fast as I could so as not to be sent rolling about the cabin as were all my goods and chattels but when eventually the squirrels in their heavy cage were pitched headlong into the fray I felt bound to go to their rescue; however it was little I could do, I was in such a miserable plight myself, even though not *very sick.* The doctor ordered me champagne and for some days I had to take it.

When we got out of the Gulf Stream we had hail and snow and the sea continuing pretty rough all the way, but one gets seasoned enough to it to get up and go about and we braved the cold on deck for the sake of the moonlight which we had for two or three nights, the "unsociable Captain" making himself quite agreeable.

On Friday morning to the delight of all we sighted land, and in the evening we landed mails outside the harbor of Queenstown. It was 5 P.M. on Saturday and getting dusk when the "Tender" bringing the Customs officers and passengers's friends came alongside the Russia and as I looked on I wished so much I had someone to help me in the coming struggle and regretted I had done nothing in the matter, when all at once my eyes were gladdened by the sight of Mr. Rathbone's servant who had recognized me and was holding up a packet of letters. In a few minutes he was on board and a load was taken off my shoulders. The packet contained letters from Miss T, Mrs. Pares, Mrs. Paget, Mrs. Hamilton and Mr. Rathbone—all congratulating me on my return and containing invitations. Mr. Rathbone made a point of my going straight to Allerton, which I did and OH! the haven of rest that bright comfortable house with its air of refinement seemed to me after the turmoil and tossing I had been going through. The squirrels too were made very welcome by three pretty fresh looking girls in white dresses and blue ribbons—Ella, Hilda and Minna Rathbone, the latter about six months older than Elinor. At this pretty place I spent two days, and then came *here* for the purpose of seeing the lawyers and having a good rest. I think it was very clever of my friends to manage that their letters should reach me, and of course Mrs. Paget was their mainstay, she having interest at Liverpool. I am trying to find an escort for the squirrels as until I do they tie me. Next week I go to Hopwell. It looked so well as I passed it the other day. It stands well on its elevated site, with its fine woods stretching around it, and is seen for some distance. The squirrels are dear.

I shan't write again for sometime unless on business.

Ever your affectionate mother,
Harriette Pares

In a few days another letter concerning the squirrels was written by Mrs. Pares, this one to her other daughter. The Humberstone mentioned in it was the country house of the Pagets, for whose daughter the squirrels were intended.

Hopwell Hall
Derbyshire, England
November 9, 1875

My dearest Alice:

I came here on the 1st, as soon as I could after sending off the squirrels. *They* had to travel to town in charge of the guard, their mistress sending to meet them; and *such* a welcome as they received. Nina wrote that not only would they find a "mother" but an "affectionate family." I was getting quite fond of them myself and missed them much, but of course they were a tie. T. Paget asked me to Humberstone, ditto the squirrels on whose account I declined to do more than to go to the theatre on the Saturday and spend Sunday at Humberstone—I am going to stay there when I leave this place. Thomas Henry was most anxious for us ladies to meet the shooting party at the Swiss Hut today for luncheon, but we one and all thought it too cold. I fancy they are having great sport as we heard of 40 brace of pheasants having been bagged before ½ past eleven. . . .

On a recent trip to London, Wright wrote me that he had looked up the house at Number 2, The Boltons, in Kensington where Beatrix Potter lived as a child and saw across the green from it Number 28, which was the house of Nina Paget. The girls were friends. In *The Journal of Beatrix Potter, 1881–1890*, the young diarist tells of the sad fate of a guinea pig that was lent her by Nina Paget. But the squirrels' arrival in the Paget household, and their temporary transfer to Mistress Potter across the green, along with the events that may have happened to them under her stewardship there, apparently occurred too early to be included in the journal.

I, too, when last in London, went to The Boltons, an oval stretch of turf off Brompton Road, to see the houses. There were gray squirrels on the green there and in the trees. But when I asked one whether it had any genes from the onetime pets in Number 28, it wouldn't tell me.

Beatrix Potter, whose books (starting with *The Tale of Peter Rabbit*) must still annually sell almost as well as The Bible, wrote two books about squirrels. The first, *Squirrel Nutkin*, was about a red squirrel. The second, *The Tale of Timmy Tiptoes*, was about a gray squirrel. It seems indisputable that the first gray squirrels Miss Potter ever laid eyes on were those that arrived in the Paget digs across the green late in 1875—a pair of New Yorkers, it seems plain enough, since they were collected in that city—Nina Paget's coddled and cosseted dar- 69 lings that could well have been the inspiration for the eventual Timmy Tiptoes.

While squirrel pets were common for many years in Great Britain both early and later, they were by no means uncommon in this country, as a number of letters in my files testify. An early example is to be found in the Washington wing of the Winterthur Museum of the Du Pont family, outside Wilmington, Delaware. A portrait of Benjamin Badger of Boston, done about 1750–60, shows a pet squirrel beside the subject. A letter from Bern, Switzerland, tells of a later pet:

"I thought you might be interested to hear of my experiences with a young squirrel. When I was somewhere in the vicinity of twelve years old, I came into possession of a baby squirrel that had been found on the grounds of a grade school in my hometown of Augusta, Georgia. With my mother's assistance, I fed the squirrel with milk from an eyedropper and it thrived and was soon able to take more solid nourishment. It was eventually necessary to remove the squirrel (I'm certain it had a name, but am shocked to realize I can't recall it) to a large, wire-fronted cage outdoors. Although the cage contained a segment of tree branch on which the squirrel could climb around, I often took him out and allowed him to climb to the tops of trees, some of them oaks taller than our three-story house. I also took the squirrel inside, where he enjoyed climbing to the tops of the draperies; this outlet for his recreational needs was terminated when my mother objected to his chewing the wallpaper around the window sills. Whether indoors or out, the squirrel never failed to return to my custody and allow himself to be returned to his cage."

An unusual pet of recent times was a squirrel that was led on a golden leash through Central Park in the early thirties. An even more unusual one was Skippy. It belonged to Ted Townsend. He was the famous New York State game warden of Westchester County. His was a name to conjure with in Eastern natural-history circles almost from the time he took the job in 1916 to the middle of this century. It was said of him that New York City was bounded on the east by Connecticut, on the south by the Atlantic Ocean, on the west by New Jersey, and on the north by Ted Townsend who, his intimates averred, was fluent in the language of many animals and birds, speaking fox, pheasant, deer, robin, and duck perfectly, and warbler with only a slight human accent, its thin, high notes being a bit troublesome for him. Once, while demonstrating his talent to a companion, Townsend's vigorous and repeated kak-kak-kak's brought a cock pheasant virtually to his shoe tops before he dismissed it with a clap of his hands.

"What in God's name did you say to the bird?" his friend asked.

"Come closer," Townsend answered.

Another time he calmed perturbed residents of Ardsley-on-Hudson by exactly mimicking the weird nocturnal cries that had so

agitated them. "A mother fox mourning her grown-up cubs' departure," Townsend said. "She'll soon stop."

Skippy, the squirrel pet of this accomplished linguist, lived in a box on the Townsend kitchen floor. A dentist from time to time worked on its teeth to prevent them from growing too backward. Skippy had a bad case of malocclusion. Its incisors were so poorly aimed that they couldn't keep each other ground down when it gnawed, as they were supposed to. Skippy was enormously fond of television. When Townsend turned on the set, it deserted the box on the kitchen floor and perched contentedly on his shoulder. Skippy was especially interested in wrestling matches, making soft, satisfied sounds as the large, beefy antagonists flung each other about. However, an opposite mood occurred when Mrs. Townsend pressed her husband's trousers in the kitchen. Then Skippy had to be sent from the room. Otherwise it became frantic and raced around the kitchen, scolding volubly. It was Townsend's theory that Skippy had a protective attitude toward him, and that the squirrel believed the trousers were part of his pelt.

5. THE SQUIRREL
AS MENACE

The gray squirrel has a large ego, and consequently it is an opinionated and self-seeking mammal. The statement of a naturalist that "a three- or four-year-old squirrel is the unquestioned master of almost any situation it is apt to confront" seems to fit it nicely. The largely successful pursuit of its own ends sometimes brings the gray into conflict with man. Man, when his wishes are transgressed by his furry friend, suffers a medley of emotions—surprised disbelief, admiring laughter, grumpy annoyance, and even intense squirrel hatred. Sometimes, to those of us afflicted with squirrel problems, squirrels seem to appear not only where squirrels might be expected to appear but everywhere—on rooftops, begonia beds, highways, and kitchen porches, among others. As one victim feelingly observed, "It is a raider of gardens, a despoiler of the homes of nesting birds, and a past master at satisfying its own omnivorous wants—although personally charming, God damn him." Of course, from the squirrel's point of view, it's a completely different cup of tea. Man's attitude must seem silly, if not venally ungenerous.

The three most common complaints against *Sciurus carolinensis* 73 are the robbing of bird feeders, the invasion of houses, and the interruption of electric power and telephone service. Of course, there are many other kinds of complaints.

I think it can be said without fear of contradiction that one of the greatest problems of those who feed birds is keeping squirrels out of the feeders, those (for the squirrels) veritable cornucopias that enliven the winter scene. My own experience is a good example. I once lived in a wooded area of New York's Westchester County. Winter birds and squirrels were numerous there. Knowing the proclivities of the latter, I erected a platform feeder atop a thin, vertical, ten-foot metal pole embedded in the ground. The pipe's smooth surface, I thought, would prevent the squirrels from mounting it. Not at all. They went up it as though they were strolling level ground. Considerably miffed, I applied a generous coating of automotive grease to the pole in an effort to thwart them. To no avail. In some fiendishly clever manner, they were able to press against the pole with their pads and reach the feeder, but just how I was never able to discover.

A more noticeably acrobatic performance was relayed to me in a letter from a gentleman on the West Coast, recounting a Midwestern experience. He said:

"I have a true squirrel story that I think will interest you.

"My daughter Bess and her husband John Ross and family live in their home in Madison, Wisconsin. The rear of the house borders on a green belt of trees in a ravine. They had trouble with the squirrels eating all the food out of the bird feeders. John rigged a cord and pulleys extending from the rail of their upper-level porch to one of the big trees about 40 feet away. The bird feeder hung from this cord, could be pulled to the porch for replenishing and returned to the center for the birds.

"While we were there Thanksgiving Day, we all watched a surprise performance by a big gray squirrel. He leaped from an upper limb of the tree to the cord, reaching it about 20 feet from the feeder. He hung upside down on the cord and propelled himself rapidly to

the feeder using his feet so nimbly and rapidly, he seemed to be running although upside down. After enjoying the feeder, if we came onto the porch, he leaped to a lower limb and when we disappeared, he would climb to a higher limb and repeat the performance.

"It all seemed so natural and easy for him. One certainly marvels at how he could plan such a feat. We were all entertained for our Thanksgiving party.

"Have you ever witnessed a comparable stunt?"

I haven't, but Mrs. Judith Smith, of Newell Farm, West Newbury, Massachusetts, has. She wrote me:

"I have a small item to share. Several years ago my father was given a 'squirrel gym' as a present because he enjoyed watching the squirrels year round. The gym consisted of a clothesline with about four hanging plastic cups in which to put nuts. We strung it in the front yard. The squirrels soon caught on. They would start out from the top of the line but soon swing under and move along out to the cups. Then they had to hang by their hind feet to reach the cups and nuts."

These, however, by no means cover all instances of squirrel ingenuity. They are determined problem solvers, as the following stories indicate. The first is a communication from Dr. Daniel Leavitt of Roanoke, Virginia:

"A few additional notes on squirrels. These animals are getting entirely too proficient in finding the solutions. After man has extinguished himself, they will take over, viz—

"For the past few years we have had a satellite bird feeder. This is a plastic globe that hangs by a long thin steel wire about eight feet above the ground. For all this time the squirrels have been satisfied with what the birds drop. This year a new squirrel appeared, gray with a slight red tint on the back. He studied the problem for weeks. Finally he hung head down, grasped the wire and slid down. When he reached the feeder he was going too fast, fell off and hit the ground. Over the next two weeks he learnt to slow up, how I don't know, and at last was hanging upside down above the feeder. The opening was too small to put his head in, but he could put in one forepaw, stuff his mouth and drop off. This satisfied him for a week and then he gnawed the opening so that he could get his head in. My wife was determined that she was not going to support beggars as there were plenty of nuts in the trees so I moved the feeder. This time I hung the feeder from a branch thirty feet up by a fifteen-foot thin cord. He solved this one in a day. He chewed through the cord where it crossed the branch, the feeder fell and he went down and cleaned it out. Score—squirrel–2, Leavitts–0."

This next testimony, which enlarges on the notable adaptability described above, is from a magazine clipping sent me by a Pennsylvania resident. The substance of the item is as follows:

A woman at a fashionable New York shop bought a supposedly squirrel-proof bird feeder. May the smooth-talking salesman, she said, "stagnate in Macy's forever!"

At first, all went well. But then word got around among the squirrels about this challenging food container and many gathered, looking up at the feeder which hung from a tree branch outside the house. In particular, one big gray worked on the knotty problem. "The gray was an acrobat, high diver and long jumper, a Flying Wallenda among squirrels," the woman said. "His first few approaches were unsuccessful. He attempted to pull the feeder up to the branch but found it too heavy. Then he tried descending the rope headfirst, but the opening nearest the top remained just out of reach. Once he lost his grip on the rope and took a header into the snow. 'Give it up, dummy,' I cackled from behind the window. He chattered at me furiously and kept on trying.

"Finally, one morning I arose to discover that the feeder was almost empty, though I had filled it only the night before. I refilled it and waited. Before long I spotted Big Gray scampering in the branches overhead and he was poised directly above the feeder. Continuously descending the rope hind legs first, he grasped the handle attached to the feeder's cover with the toes of his hind feet, and hung upside down. In this position, he could reach the three top openings. My birdseed bill doubled, then tripled."

Perhaps better than either of the foregoing, the next instance illustrates the squirrel's tenacity, determination, and brain power. It came to me in a letter from a professor of zoology at the University of California at Davis. The professor said:

"Here is an addition to your collection of squirreliana:

"Eiseley, Loren C. The Fire Apes. *Harper's,* Sept. 1949. In which the distinguished former Provost of the University of Pennsylvania recounts *his* experience with a Supersquirrel at a bird feeder, and its implications for human evolution."

The former provost said, in part in paraphrase: My bird-feeding station was on a lawn, erected by the former owner to baffle squirrels. A little wooden platform under a roof was on a thin, smooth pipe [much like mine had been]. But the pipe was topped by half an inverted metal bread box to keep the squirrels away. It was placed so no squirrel could spring across from a nearby tree.

As Eiseley was sitting in the garden one morning, he saw five squirrels try to solve the puzzle. They knew food was aloft. But how to reach it? They went up the thin pipe only to find the tin shield balked them. They slid protestingly back to earth, and tried to ignore the provost's chuckles. Attempting to preserve their dignity, they retreated with a completely unsuccessful show of indifference.

Then came a sixth squirrel. Eiseley was bored by then and almost asleep.

"God knows how many things a man misses by becoming smug. . . . I almost drowsed enough to miss it. . . . If I had. . . . I might even have died, believing some crass anthropocentric dogma about the uniqueness of the human brain.

"As it was, I had just one sleepy eye half open, and it was through that that I saw the end of humanity. It was really a little episode, and if it hadn't been for the squirrel I wouldn't have seen it at all. The thing was this: he stopped to think. He stopped right there at the bottom of the pole and looked up and I knew he was thinking. Then he went up.

"He went up with a bound that swayed the thin pipe slightly and teetered the loose shield. In practically the next second he had caught the tilted rim of the shield with an outstretched paw, flicked his body onto and over it, and was sitting on the platform where only birds were supposed to sit. He dined well there and daintily. . . ."

Although the Roanoke medical doctor and the Pennsylvania doctor of philosophy both make the point that the squirrel might take over our orb because it is so successful in robbing our bird feeders, I sense that the remarks are poetic exaggeration to emphasize the intelligence of the squirrel. And it is well, perhaps, to emphasize that point. It seems fair to say this to all owners of squirrel-proof bird feeders: They may work for a time. But don't become too confident. Tomorrow that may change. Tomorrow may arrive the conqueror, the furry Einstein of the out-of-doors.

Many victimized owners of bird feeders will be glad to know that squirrels do not always get the best of birds. A woman who feeds birds in her meadow at Cape Ann, Massachusetts, had great trouble with squirrels. They drove off her chosen guests and stole their food until a savior arrived—a male pheasant that, with beak open in threat, stood his ground before the filchers and routed them. And in matters of territoriality, so important to animals, at least one bird wins consistent victories over a squirrel. A nuclear physicist in the District of Columbia tells me that in his backyard is a holly tree much desired as a perch by both a gray squirrel and a blue jay. Vociferous battles erupt when both are on the scene together. But invariably the blue jay, by darting with sharp beak at the squirrel's eyes, drives it out and the squirrel, chattering angrily, retreats to a nearby oak.

Nearby trees are what cause the second problem, mentioned earlier, to householders. Squirrels in town and suburbia have an undeniable attraction to homes. Nearby trees are their usual bridge to them. Houses seem to squirrels a naturally available shelter from wind and rain, from the snow and winter chill.

A writer colleague of mine realized this only too well. Long a homeowner in Brooklyn, he had for many years a running battle with squirrels in his attic. Nothing seemed to work. A prized tree standing in his yard provided easy access to the roof. Once there, the squirrels would gnaw through the shingles, or the wood under the eaves, to reach their goal, the cozy attic. From time to time, my friend would give me bulletins. No counter-ploy seemed to help. Such obnoxious smelly substances as mothballs or moth flakes liberally sprinkled over the top floor did no good. Neither did sulfur candles or pieces of cloth soaked in one of the recently developed animal repellents. The last time I saw him, he said resignedly, "The squirrels   79 won." After a bit of interrogation, he told me he had sold the house in Brooklyn and moved to an apartment in Manhattan, putting his squirrel troubles forever behind him. "What about the squirrels?" I asked. "The new owner has ousted them," he said. "He did what I wouldn't do; he cut down the tree."

Such contiguous trees have for years generated countless confrontations, not only with squirrels versus people, but people versus people. Some of the last end up in court. An example occurred in Westchester a while back. A couple in a home next to a neighbor's large cherry tree were visited by squirrels that moved along its branches to *their* roof. For a couple of years the afflictees endeavored to get the cherry-tree owners to lop the offending branches. Finally they haled them to court. The judge, after hearing the evidence, held with due gravity that the plaintiffs had indeed a case.

The most horrendous house occupation that I know of took place some thirty miles south of the cherry-tree incident in Far Rockaway, a pleasant outer section of New York City. The seizure was not instantaneous; it took a while to develop. Half a decade earlier a squirrel with furry grace leaped from the branches of an oak nearby onto the roof of the large colonial stone and stucco house. Things went beautifully for a time. The house owners happily fed and observed the visitor. But, in due course, it invited friends. Within several years, the state of affairs had done a complete turnabout. The squirrel population around the house had risen dramatically, as squirrel populations have been known to do. Within five years from the date of the first arrival, squirrels were on every floor. In the face of a mobile, bewhiskered army, the beleaguered householders called frantically for public assistance.

Only the previous week the roof had been repaired. Now rain was coming in again. The shingling resembled a sieve. The invaders had eaten a cake in the kitchen. They had bitten holes in the dining-room tablecloth. They had destroyed a valuable Persian rug. The day of the complaint one had crawled down the wife's back. "We're really crazy with them," the victim said. A terrier they had bought to rout the trespassers had proved ineffective. As it rushed about the house barking, the squirrels retreated, only to reappear in its absence. The couple were in a quandary. They believed that chemicals strong enough to dislodge the squirrels would harm them and the dog; to kill the squirrels outright, they knew was illegal. So they appealed to the state.

When accounts of the problem appeared in the papers, the troubled couple had only further botheration. For a week, they were harassed by letters, phone calls, and curious motorists come to see the squirrels. A man in Georgia wrote a letter of sympathy saying that squirrels had destroyed his grove of almond trees. A California woman temporarily in New York City said she would take any squirrels that were apprehended. Phone callers by the dozen asked that one of the squirrels be saved for them. A woman in Brooklyn wrote that "Squirrels are very cute little animals and you should be glad you have them with you." A Manhattan woman said she would give ten cents for every squirrel caught, which she would transport to an area with a dearth of squirrels.

The episode had a happy ending, particularly for the squirrels. After considerable indecision on the part of the authorities, and the passage of a fortnight, a game warden live-trapped the troop and removed them bodily to the sylvan confines of Brooklyn's Prospect Park, where there were other things than shingled roofs, tablecloths, and Persian rugs to engage their attention. Presumably they lived there happily ever after.

Although individuals can suffer annoyance and pecuniary loss through the acts of miscreant squirrels, unquestionably the damage done by them that affects the largest number of people—and the total affected can run into the tens of thousands—is the interruption of electric power and/or telephone service. This they do by biting the overhead lines, or causing short-circuits of the lines or of electric generators, or otherwise tampering with apparatus that shouldn't   81 concern them. Sometimes, but not always, it costs them their lives.

The public prints regularly carry stories like these from the not-too-distant past:

SQUIRREL IN JERSEY
CUTS POWER SUPPLY
FOR 35,000 USERS

Clifton, N.J., Nov. 13—A squirrel switched off electrical current for 35,000 customers of the Public Service Electric and Gas Company today.

The power failure at the Athenia switching station began at 8:04 A.M. when the squirrel pushed a disconnect button atop a steel tower, controlling a 26,000-volt line, a company spokesman said. The squirrel was badly scorched and died, he added.

Public Service engineers, puzzled by the failure and unaware of its cause, checked lines and circuits and finally got the power back at 8:17 A.M.

Service to parts of Passaic, Clifton, Lodi, Garfield, Wallington, Rutherford and East Rutherford was cut. Thousands of homes were without electricity and several industries were stilled.

At the Weston Biscuit Company, 2 Brighton Avenue, Passaic, several thousand pounds of cookies burned up in ovens. Among them were governmental survival biscuits for fallout shelters.

The cookies travel through high-temperature ovens on steel belts. When the power went off, the belts stopped, leaving the cookies in the oven. The gas in the ovens shut off automatically but the heat remained at 600 to 700 degrees for a long period.

The power failure lit the entire alarm board at the Passaic Fire Department Headquarters as alarm systems automatically were activated. No alarms were genuine, Fire Department officials said.

Or:

STATEN ISLAND SQUIRRELS
LOSE POWER STRUGGLE

Staten Island squirrels have apparently met defeat in a war with Consolidated Edison customers and officials.

For some time the squirrels had been getting into live electrical equipment at Con Ed substations, causing thousands of dollars in damage and power failures.

On one occasion the rodents knocked out the power for 3,000 families and another time left 1,000 customers without electricity, according to a utility spokesman.

Then traps were set at all substations in the borough with peanut butter as the bait. Captured squirrels are released in wooded areas. The traps have so far proved successful.

Following up on the last item, I learned from the utility in Staten Island, the most rural of New York City's five boroughs, that the substations were locations where very high voltage from generators was cut to lower levels preparatory to further reduction at pole-top transformers. The bare metal cables that carry the high voltage are screened in the substations from human contact. But the squirrels had no difficulty infiltrating the substations, easily climbing the protective fences and scampering over the floors amid the high-voltage lines. When they would touch one with part of their body while another part touched the floor, they would short out the line and themselves to boot.

Peanut butter is high on the list of squirrel yummies. A plethora of peanut-butter-baited traps, strategically placed and watched, seems to have corrected the Staten Island situation.

83

Besides touching bare wires or pushing buttons, squirrels are frequently seen to bite overhead lines, which are most often sheathed with lead. As a result, sometimes power goes out or telephone service is disturbed. These problems have existed ever since overhead lines became common almost a century ago. Because of the persistence of the problems, a widespread belief has long prevailed among power people that a squirrel's diet includes lead and other forms of metal. Many approaches have been devised in attempts to protect the overhead lines. One is given in the letter of a gentleman from California:

"At a cocktail party in Mt. Carroll, Illinois, in the '50's I met a man from Bell Telephone who claimed to be in charge of research on squirrels chewing holes in the lead sheath covering telephone lines. The problem, he said, was that the little buggers would bite holes in the protective covering—the lead—and rain, snow, dew, frost would seep into the holes and short out the wiring. He had, he said, spent two years experimenting with chemical deterrents. Quinine-flavored lead, licorice-flavored lead, etc., all dead ends.

"But, he said, in recent months he had shifted the thrust of his research to an ecological approach, mapping locations of squirrel damage, and thence to squirrel psychology. The mapping had revealed a clear pattern; within any locality, squirrel bites in the lead were at the busiest intersections.

"His response to this discovery was to station squirrel watchers at crucial corners where damage was heavy. Their reports had been consistent across the country. The phone company was hanging the operational lead-sheathed cluster of lines three or four inches below a steel weight-bearing wire. The squirrels, said his spies, were sitting, rear feet on the lower cable, front paws on the steel wire, watching the traffic with obvious pleasure. But a break in the flow of automobiles annoyed them (like a commercial break in a TV program?) and in what seemed to the observers obvious pique they would bend down and bite the lead.

"My friend of the afternoon reported that he had that morning submitted his final and triumphant recommendation to Ma Bell. Stop suspending the cable from the weight-bearing wire. Wrap the steel around the lead so as not to provide a bleacher seat for the squirrels!"

Since subsequent damage to telephone lines still occurred, perhaps the researcher's remedy was rejected or not as successful as he had hoped. A more recent solution to squirrels biting telephone lines will be mentioned shortly.

I suspect people everywhere within the gray squirrel's range have experienced occasions like the three mentioned above. My records include similar stories from the states of Connecticut, Delaware, Maryland, Massachusetts, Mississippi, New Hampshire, Pennsylvania, South Carolina, and Virginia.

An aura of mystery has sometimes surrounded the squirrel and electricity. People see the squirrel walking unharmed along naked overhead high-voltage wires and wonder how safe this is. Birds, too, they notice, perch on the lines without damage. Survival is possible, however, only so long as the squirrel does not become part of a circuit. It is safe, so long as it walks along the wire. But let its tail drop and touch a second bare wire below and its body then becomes part of a circuit. A short occurs and the squirrel is electrocuted. The same thing happens if a bird, especially a big bird like a golden eagle, perches on a bare high-voltage wire as they often do in the West. Then, if it lets its wings droop and touch the metal, the result is the same as above. In summary, an animal is electrocuted when part of its body comes in contact with the conductor of an electric current and another part of its body then comes into contact with a second conductor or with the ground or with a conductor that is connected with the ground.

Often, of course, as has been mentioned, a squirrel walks along a *covered* overhead line carrying electricity. Then the animal, seemingly driven by a perverse appetite that baffles and infuriates installers and maintenance men, may bite into the sheath of lead or other material covering the line. If there is a strong current in the   85 line, a short can occur. But more often the sheath is merely punctured. If it is a telephone wire, messages going over it will at least crackle disconcertingly. However, even with the merest impairment of audibility, complaints, understandably, arise.

A few months ago, the papers in New York City carried a lengthy account of squirrel damage to telephone lines and the uproar by subscribers that this occasioned. It was stated that in one seventy-block area in north Flushing in the borough of Queens, which has numerous trees, the sheathing of the lines had been bitten through in 834 places, requiring more than half of nine miles of cable to be replaced. Lines in Staten Island, southern Brooklyn, and the north Bronx also had been bitten.

One account said: "This all leads phone company engineers to make return trips to the drawing board. Put lead sheaths around the wires. The squirrels eat through the lead. Try polyethylene and they eat through polyethylene.

" 'They'll gnaw on anything,' said Bernard Stegman, of the Arrow Exterminating Company. . . .

"So Robert Dolan, telephone company engineer and his buddies are trying something else, vinyl plastic 'squirrel guards' on the remaining four miles of cable in north Flushing—the guards being so slippery it is thought even a squirrel will have a tough time grabbing hold of them—and steel sheathing on the five miles of line to be replaced."

Actually, the reason for the squirrel's biting overhead lines is simple. As is the case with other mysteries that persist for years, there is often a natural and easy explanation. The heads of businesses or industries affected by these mysteries don't bother to investigate the reasons, and even such animal experts as Warden Ted Townsend can be baffled. He had no inkling of the key to the mystery of squirrel line-biting. He often said to me, "Why squirrels crave the electrical snacks is beyond me. But occasionally they do, and then the public utility, the customers in the area, and the squirrels themselves are in trouble."

In the newspaper account quoted above, a brief unveiling of the enigma was given by a representative of the American Association for the Prevention of Cruelty to Animals. She said that the furry creatures can't stop the habit of chewing overhead wires: "Their teeth are the toughest of any animal of the diminutive persuasion, and they must constantly be ground down because they grow so quickly."

The rodents, the tribe of which the squirrel is a member, own teeth especially adapted for gnawing. These are the large, curved, deeply-rooted incisors at the front of each jaw, with the slightly larger pair in the lower jaw. The teeth are different from those of many animals because they grow continuously from the roots and must be worn away at the tips. The teeth are interesting for another reason. Enamel protects the front surfaces only so that the teeth wear faster at the back. Thus a keen edge is constantly developed, making Chiselteeth a name occasionally used by popular natural-history writers for rodents, and conferring on them the ability to cut through very hard substances.

A study of rodent teeth reports that the greatest growth so far discovered belongs to the pocket gopher, which uses the incisors for digging, entailing a lot of wear. Fourteen inches a year is their growth. That of the guinea pig is up to ten inches, the common rat up to six. That of the gray squirrel varies from six inches to considerably less than that, depending on the authority. From the socket in the jaw bone, the incisors measure more than an inch long, but stand only a fraction of that above the gum.

If the incisors of a squirrel are allowed to grow unchecked, the creature is in deep trouble. It needs to have these teeth meet to live a normal life and feed itself properly. Were the incisors not worn down by gnawing, they would continue to grow in a curved fashion, eventually penetrating the animal's upper and lower jaws if it lived that long. Consequently it bites hard substances such as lead and tough plastics, not only on overhead lines, but wherever else it can find them. It chews lead identification labels on ornamental trees or metal number tags on telephone poles to reduce tooth length. For the same reason it has chewed the toes off some lead statues in English parks, vastly incensing the walkers there. In the forests, squirrels employ the shells of defunct tortoises, the shed antlers of a buck, or the shoulder blade of a deer skeleton for the same purpose. Small bones have even been found wedged in the crotch of trees. Presumably the squirrel goes there for a therapeutic gnaw when it feels the incisors need curbing. Recent studies have also shown that squirrels grind the incisors together, in all likelihood to further the same end.

Thus the new steel cable installed by the New York Telephone Company to protect its lines in north Flushing may, as far as the squirrel is concerned, be just as useful as the softer lead in keeping its incisors in line. As for whether the vinyl plastic squirrel guard on the rest of the Flushing lines will keep the squirrels off, time will tell.

My correspondents and newspaper columns have informed me of other squirrel misdeeds.

In London, British squirrels of pure American stock showed little consideration a few years back for the garden of our Ambassador to the Court of St. James. For a while they were punished for their audacity. But in the end, as so often happens, they won the fray. The situation was this. A half mile north of the American embassy on Grosvenor Square is Winfield House, the private residence of our ambassador, then Walter Annenberg. It stands in the confines of Regent's Park, one of the city's largest, and has ample flower beds. Gardeners of the ambassador duly planted six thousand crocus bulbs on the grounds. And what happened? Gray squirrels descended en masse. They dug up bulbs and ate scores. The beds were a shambles and so was the ambassador's temper. When queried, park authorities suggested shooting. Five squirrels went down. Then, alerted by the news, London television crews made tracks for Winfield House. "Cease firing," ordered the ambassador. The squirrels were left to the run of the beds.

A somewhat similar experience befell the superintendent of Roger Williams Park in Providence, Rhode Island. His 3,500 tulip bulbs were planted deep in the earth to thwart the squirrels, but they found them and ate 1,500. The superintendent, a man evidently not wise in the ways of squirrels, was amazed. "The bulbs were six inches down in the earth," he said. "I don't know how the squirrels knew they were there. Could they have watched the workmen putting them in?" Squirrel olfactory power was crassly overlooked.

In another case, a gentleman living on the outskirts of Wilmington, Delaware, appealed to the readers of a rural magazine for suggestions as to how to preserve the apples in his small orchard of ten or twelve trees from marauding squirrels. He got a bountiful response. Recommendations included, but did not stop with, winding creosoted ropes around the tree trunks, placing moth balls all over the small plot, and playing rock music by means of a radio placed under a metal pail in the middle of the trees. One correspondent from New England begged him not to uproot his trees, as he had threatened to do, but to catch the squirrels in Havahart traps and

drag them a bit through full rain barrels before release. "That will diminish their arrogance," the writer said.

The victim observed, "By the time I had received all the advice and tried to apply the numerous recommendations, my 1975 apple crop had already been stolen by the critters. Yet I was determined not to give up."

Temporary salvation came in the form of a sticky, pastelike substance manufactured in Connecticut, and proposed to him by a lady in Vermont. It was to be spread on the trunks of the trees. Once on hands, paws, or fur, it was, said the orchardist, practically impossible to remove. Following one sniff, the squirrels avoided it like the devil does holy water. The trees carrying the repellent produced a good crop.

A year ago I reached the gentleman to inquire how his orchard was coming along. The answer was so-so. He had stopped using the repellent paste, having discovered it was bad for the trees. Nor could I, when I tried, locate the manufacturer in Connecticut. Perhaps the disadvantage mentioned had put him out of business. As nearly as I could judge from my phone conversation with the orchardist, the squirrels once more seemed to have won a battle.

The next and final episode is one of the more inexplicable in my dossier. It concerns a robbery. At least that was what it was originally called. A number of years back a couple in Roslyn, Long Island, which is located in Nassau County, returned to their home to find it broken into. Clothing was spread on the lawn. So was chinaware, some of it in pieces. Highly agitated, they called the police and reported a burglary. Furthermore, they demanded the best detectives available to solve it. But these were in Mineola, the county seat, some miles to the south. By the time the plainclothesmen arrived, the sheepish owners knew the truth. Some time after the call, squirrels, out-and-out evildoers, were found ransacking the place. They had committed the break-in. The detectives with a few grumbles went back to Mineola, the owners shooed the squirrels out of the house, and started the business of recovering and replacing their errant belongings.

How, and why, did squirrels carry coats and dresses out onto the lawn? How, and why, did they do this with dishes? The whole incident, viewed dispassionately, seems one of the greatest accomplishments of squirreldom. I do not understand it. But perhaps to be the architects of such a feat is to be beyond the understanding of ordinary men.

6. SQUIRREL PEOPLE AND ANTI-SQUIRREL PEOPLE

Though it probably can be said without contradiction that Benjamin Franklin was a squirrel person, there have been others, many of them able to show more tangible interest in the breed than an aging diplomat with manifold matters on his mind. One was the head of a Paterson, New Jersey, household. When he, his wife, and six children were told that their pet squirrel, Sleepy, was unwelcome and could no longer be kept in their housing-project apartment, they begged reconsideration of the rule barring pets. They pointed out that parakeets and goldfish were in residence, but these, management said, were allowable exceptions. The family was downcast, but defiant. "If Sleepy goes, we go, too," said the father. Whereupon all eight resolute squirrel persons, accompanied by Sleepy, moved out.

Squirrel feeders are also squirrel persons, if of a minor sort. Among them are numbered the near-sighted old lady or gentleman, about whom the tale is told, probably truthfully, that when seated on a park bench in one of our metropolises, they called blithely, "Here squirrel, squirrel, squirrel," and offered a peanut to a receptive rat.

Once in a while there looms above the horizon a squirrel feeder   93 cast in the heroic mold, a feeder who can be called an outstanding squirrel person. A humble, elderly, anonymous man of Czechoslovak origin is one such. For years not long ago he appeared early each winter morning in New York City's Madison Square Park with two plastic shopping bags full of food for the squirrels. A walk of half a mile from his home had brought him there. Often he was the only person in the park. Slowly and silently he would raise atop one of two aluminum poles that he carried a decapitated beer can full of acorns and other fare and drop it into the crotches and hollows of every large tree in the park. For extra-high locations the poles, reaching up a dozen feet, were joined. Trees lacking suitable receptacles had food sprinkled at their bases. This ever-dependable squirrel benefactor, present when all the fair-weather summer feeders were absent, never wished his name to be known.

City folk who find small baby squirrels fallen from the nest are also squirrel persons by impulse. Many telephone the American Society for the Prevention of Cruelty to Animals, asking what they should do with the foundling and/or how to raise it. ASPCA people recommend that the caller, if possible, place the baby in a safe spot where its cries will attract the mother. Rearing a baby squirrel, they say, is a matter for the dedicated. For those adamant to attempt this, the Associated Humane Society of Newark, New Jersey, has a booklet on baby squirrels; cost, one dollar. Of course, one foster parent is readily available. Mother cats whose kittens have been taken from them have no hesitancy in adopting baby squirrels. Records of such adoptions, including newspaper photographs of the satisfied nursing mother, are numerous.

Squirrel watchers are also squirrel persons, if often only passive ones—although the zeal and perseverance with which some follow this diversion might make passive seem too pallid a word. As dedicated an animal lover as Cleveland Amory, founder of the Fund for Animals, who has harsh words for those who do not view the world of animals with his own humane consideration, was asked "What kind of animals do you most like to watch?" "This is going to surprise you," Amory replied, "but I am going to pick squirrels," a compliment, indeed, from one who knows, more or less, the antics of most species.

Motion seems the great attraction. Often squirrels appear unable to be still for more than a few moments at a time. Their characteristic activity, vocal and physical, charms watchers. The gray-coats race across the ground. Dash up tree trunks. Propel themselves from tipmost top to tipmost top, a phantom on a branch, a shimmer in the sun, pausing only momentarily from time to time to give a passing dog or pedestrian a piece of their mind.

Pranksters, acrobats, revelers, they can invent the liveliest game of tag ever seen. Autumn dashes through leafless trees. Swift sprints along budding boughs of springtime, the pursued and the pursuer barely a breath apart. Each movement a ripple of sleek agility, twig-borne balance a constant defial of the parlous and perilous, the whole an example of precarious perfection. Suddenly the pursued becomes the pursuer. And so the game goes on.

A woman in Central Park whom I had often seen watching the squirrels would be at it day after day, radiating the while a quiet satisfaction. I approached her one afternoon and we began squirrel talk. She said that every fine afternoon she would exercise by walking in the park and cleanse the cobwebs from her brain by watching the squirrels. "Did you ever see such agility?" she asked. "Yet they are by no means entirely safe from falling. Still, when they seem about to, they almost always contrive to catch hold somewhere, sometimes by only a single toe. Then, with that, they lift the body up and dash onward. I don't know what I'd do without my squirrels. They seem to get the most fun from running along the narrow shoots. Sometimes they spring with the strong hind legs across open spaces, legs and tail spread out to assist the glide.

"And the tail!" the woman continued. "See that one up there, saucing its friend, the tail going from side to side in a flurry. Yet so gracefully. The most accomplished court dowager in the palace at Versailles in the Court of Louis Fourteenth could never handle her fan more elegantly, more artistically, than a squirrel does its tail."

But by no means all of the human race watch, and love, squirrels. Anti-squirrel people abound. One who lived in White Plains, New York, stood up to be counted. He did so through a response—more accurately a tirade—directed against an editorial in the paper, obviously penned by a squirrel person.

Headed "Our Obnoxious Squirrels," the letter read : "Whoever wrote the editorial 'The Romantics' must live in a cloistered area (an apartment, no doubt) and on occasion strolls over to the park to observe 'the gray squirrels dashing from tree to tree, limb to limb, acting coy and eager.' He says these destructive, gnawing rodents 'are romantics.' How naive.

"Where I live in Westchester, with matured maple trees, apple trees, and shrubbery, the squirrel is a pesky demon. He has caused me nearly $1,500 in damages, eating huge holes in the cedar-planked gables of our home. In one short weekend the mischievous pests ate a 9-by-18-inch hole through one-inch boards. Their sharp teeth perform like powerful augers. Now we have installed an expensive vinyl covering over the gables, supposedly impervious to the attacks of these obnoxious creatures.

"There is no recovery from insurance underwriters. They aver the squirrel is 'in the classification of domesticated animals.' This is an insult to the average person with the least intellect. Squirrels are predatory. They rob. They invade. They destroy. They are ravishing rodents. Laws should be amended to legalize approved methods to destroy these wily villains of property. In two years I have transported over thirty of them to country woods, trapped in humane cages.

"Romanticists? Balderdash! Sentimentally mawkish."

This diatribe did not go unanswered. It was quickly followed in the paper by a strong apologia from a woman in the neighboring community of Scarsdale. In reply, she said: "I am writing to answer the letter, 'Our Obnoxious Squirrels.' I am a 'romantic' and am not 'cloistered' in an apartment. I also live in a home in Westchester,

surrounded by many trees and many squirrels, and have never had one penny of damage done to me by them. If the gentleman who wrote the letter would invest 39¢ every so often for a bag of peanuts to feed the squirrels, maybe his problem would be over. He would have 'pets' instead of 'pests.' "

Whether the anti-squirrel correspondent from White Plains lived on Wyanoke Street, I know not. But some time ago the residents along that street comprised a solid coterie of anti-squirrel people. The cause was a squirrel that attacked them on the sidewalk, scratching and biting their arms. They appealed to the police for leave to shoot their attacker, which often lay in ambush for them. Their requests were referred to Game Warden Ted Townsend. His reaction was predictable. "Anyone," he thundered, "who shoots a squirrel out of season will feel the full effects of the law." Since the time was early summer, the eccentric creature was not shot.

In extenuation of the squirrel, it might be pointed out that its peculiar behavior began only after having been hit on the noggin by a pellet from a boy's BB gun. Presumably the irate victim, incensed by such treatment, sought vengeance.

Another individual with an anti-squirrel bent was one of my correspondents from New Hampshire. He was angry with squirrels for robbing and destroying his wife's baited bird trap that she employed to catch and band birds. So he rigged up a high-powered electric circuit to include the trap. When he saw a squirrel attempting to seize the bait or trap, he turned on the power. He wrote, I'm afraid with some relish, "It is astonishing how high a squirrel can jump from absolute zero."

Applause for this statement would doubtless come from those myriads of bird lovers whose feeders are so consistently pilfered. While I cannot condone heavy shocks to a squirrel, using relatively harmless currents to protect feeders seems natural. An architect I knew in Westchester, a technically adept man, had a lovely elevated bird-feeding station back of his residence. Because of repeated forays, he connected the feeder to a circuit capable of carrying a light electrical charge. This he turned on only when he saw squirrel robbers appearing. Before long, they showed up less and less.

A few years ago the Savings Bank Association of the State of New York became anti-squirrel. It hired a large, reputable, and notably effective advertising agency, to wit, Benton & Bowles, to devise a statewide campaign whereby the association planned to climb to eminence on the slender shoulders of the squirrel. The resultant ad showed a large picture of the animal. "He's a fraud!" the headline clamored. The point the campaign was making was that, although the squirrel often hid his savings in the form of excess food in a tree or under the ground, the little dummy forgot where they were cached. People, on the other hand, wise people, knew better. They cannily put their savings in a bank, whose location, presumably, would not slip their minds.

In a matter of hours, the Savings Bank Association of the State of New York caught it full in the chops. Defenders of Bannertail arose from all corners of the landscape. Their communications were virulent. The association should be ashamed of itself.

"Must you pick on the helpless to appear big and wise?" one reader wrote.

"You can think of something better than this to advertise, can't you?" another said.

"Really—how unfair to the helpless squirrel!" were the words a third correspondent flung at the bankers.

Nor did it stop there. A newspaper in Wilton, Connecticut, took up arms in behalf of the squirrel. "Who's a Fraud?" the headline on its editorial text asked. "We are quite mad at the Savings Bank Association of the State of New York," the item stated. It proceeded, quite rightly, to point out that people, too, forget where they put their money. What about the many unclaimed accounts so often advertised?

"You should stop picking on the poor squirrels," the editorial continued. "Chide, instead, those boobs who can't remember where their own money is."

And so it went. A full month after the ad appeared, letters, postcards, and phone calls were still coming in. Not one was complimentary to the banks and those who run them. The association and its thoroughly chastened henchman, Benton & Bowles, went into conference. Into the ring came the towel. A conciliatory statement followed to the effect that it was nice to know that people read ads, and that squirrels were really savers, even if they might not be the wisest kind of savers.

With that, both organizations on the receiving end hoped that peace would descend, and both doubtless made a mental note never—but NEVER—again to publicly slur squirrels.

It might be well to point out here that some French bankers take an entirely different view of the squirrel's prudence. Last winter in Paris I clipped from my copy of *Le Monde* a quarter-page financial ad. It was devoted to the thriftiness of the squirrel, in whose name a high-interest opportunity was offered. The ad's headline asked simply (before going into details of a delectable, tax-free, high-interest return): Do You Have a Squirrel Account in the National Savings Bank? At the bottom of the ad was a flattering, unmistakable likeness of a perky squirrel.

Among the anti-squirrel people is one who seems to have had a psychological quirk. At any rate, he was arrested—and properly so, I think—for his acts. He was a fifty-year-old carpenter from The Bronx. Sundays he would regularly appear in Central Park. Carrying a long branch festooned with fruit and nuts, he would wave it temptingly at the squirrels. When they tried to reach the food, he would jerk the branch away. Finally, to the satisfaction of other park visitors, he was arrested. The charge: harassing and tantalizing the squirrels. In court, he said he loved squirrels. Often, he said, he fed them normally. But he could offer no explanation of his Sunday conduct. He was given a fine, a caution, and a suspended sentence.

Another anti-squirrel person, however, made no bones about his feelings, although he didn't, I think, take a logical look at them. He was one of my correspondents and lived in Wilmette, Illinois. He wrote: "Has your study of squirrels found the answer to what is the value of same (squirrels) in Nature's plan? Birds eat annoying, over-abundant bugs, etc. What do squirrels do besides bury nuts? Have asked people this for years. But no answers." My quibble with his approach is this. Did the gentleman ask *himself*: What value have *I* in Nature's plan?

Reverting now to squirrel persons, I come to the most remarkable—nay, unexampled—squirrel person who has so far swum into my ken. He is William James Stillman, artist, journalist, and diplomat, an important figure in our country's nineteenth-century literary and artistic circles. He was an extremely engaging personality, and not only to squirrels. Here is what James Russell Lowell, himself a distinguished critic and outstanding poet of the period, had to say about Stillman in a letter to him:

"I'm glad you had a pleasant time here. I had, and you made me fifteen years younger while you stayed. When a man gets to my age, enthusiasms don't often knock at the door of his garret. I am all the more charmed with them when they come. A youth full of such pure intensity of hope and faith and purpose, what is he but the breath of a resurrection trumpet to us stiffened old fellows, bidding us up out of our clay and earth if we would not be too late?

"Your inspiration is still to you a living mistress; make her immortal in her promptings and her consolations by imaging her truly in art. Mine looks at me with eyes of pale flame, and beckons across a gulf. You come into my loneliness like an incarnate inspiration. And it is dreary enough sometimes; for a mountain peak on whose snow your foot makes the first mortal print is not so lonely as a room full of happy faces from which one is missing forever."

Stillman kept squirrels as pets, beginning when he was very young. Of them, he says, "In the range of my own studies of animals, in a state of nature, the squirrel has given me the greatest evidence of the capacity for *humanization* and, at the same time, of such intellectual powers as are within the limited range of the creatures we call brute."

Stillman saw a likeness to the human hand in the squirrel's forepaws—in their flexibility and handiness. One of his squirrel pets had a passion for tea. Loved it sweet and steaming. It would plunge its nose into a cup when hot enough to scald. Stillman could never account for this taste. Nor can I, never having heard of another with it.

Stillman also said, "I think the history of my squirrels, and of several others I know of, proves the capacity of the squirrel for a measure of devotion and teachableness of which few people have   101 any conception, and should the domestication become practical, the development through heredity suggests the possibility of a race of companions to man of a most fascinating quality."

Finally Stillman said it was the squirrel and the squirrel alone that "made me understand God and our place in God's creation."

Stillman also believed that squirrels had immortality.

There's a squirrel person for you.

7. LETTERS

A number of those who wrote me started their letters suggesting that perhaps I had touched a responsive chord in the squirrel-conscious public, the dimensions of which would surprise me—that, in fact, the reaction to my articles might overwhelm me.

Here is a sample of these remarks, beginning with one from a gentleman in New England: "You opened up quite a box of tacks with your articles. Like people hunting ancestors, you'll have to take what you get."

One from a man in Canada: "I imagine that by now you are reconciled to becoming the repository of rather more squirrel lore than you really need."

Another from one in Massachusetts: "I assume from your published words that your interest in the field is insatiable."

From a gentleman on the West Coast: "Such a flood of memories were released by your articles, and I was astonished by them to find that I had been all these years a closet squirrel person."

And this from a woman in Texas: "It does seem, Mr. Kinkead, that you have started the National Movement of Squirrel Watchers."

I am indeed impressed with these sentiments. Perhaps I should continue this section with the words: "All hail, National Movement of Squirrel Watchers!"

To reply to the thoughts just expressed in order of their sequence: I am entirely ready to take what I get in the way of letters; I am happy at being the repository of squirrel lore, and doubt that I will ever receive more than I really need; my interest in the subject may not be insatiable, but it borders on that; I am pleased and gratified that the closet squirrel person has finally unmasked himself; and if I have started the National Movement of Squirrel Watchers, so be it.

On the matter of tails, which are so important to squirrels, I said in one of my articles that a squirrel uses his as a sunshade in summer, a blanket in cold or stormy weather, an expressive aid in communication, a foil in skirmishes between males in the mating season, a counterbalance in effecting quick turns, as an aerial rudder when he leaps from branch to branch, and as a parachute to soften the impact of occasional falls from trees. A woman from Connecticut amplified this. She wrote: "There's another thing that squirrels do with their tails. I saw one scraping at its muzzle in a frantic little way with both paws, when it suddenly snatched up the very end of its tail and brushed it in two quick strokes across its mouth. That seemed to do it. Thus another use may be added to the squirrel's tail—that of napkin."

The intelligence of squirrels, copiously mentioned by Stillman and others, is further demonstrated in a letter from a man in Massachusetts. He had noted my remarks about Central Park squirrels avoiding traffic by various means, including sprints before sunrise across highways, and waiting by the interior roads for the traffic lights to turn red. He said: "Your essay on the squirrels of Central Park was engrossing, and it occurs to me that your many experiences and observations of them may not have included one of mine, for the very good reason that the environment of New York City does not boast the wherewithal.

"You tell of the diurnal migrations of squirrels at early morning to avoid the traffic hazard of street crossing, and quote someone as suspecting they followed traffic lights. When we lived in North Amherst, Massachusetts, where the centre consists of a wide intersection of highways, I once saw a squirrel approaching this centre running along a high utility wire along the edge of the main street. Upon arriving there, he made a right angle turn and crossed the entire intersection on a cross-wire, completely remote from, and undisturbed by, the traffic so far below him." No jaywalker that gray.

One of my Harvard correspondents, Mrs. Dorothy Kamen-Kaye, who is connected with the botany department, wrote me:

"My husband and I are 'squirrel people' and when we lived in New York became friends of many of your squirrels. We hand-fed them and I still remember those dry, hot, little paw-nails as they took the peanuts we gave them. (I'm desolated that I didn't know we ought to have offered another kind of nut.) The ones we fed looked fat and frisky. There was an old man who usually sat on a bench on the walk near the seal pool. He fed them regularly. They came and dived into his jacket pocket to get nuts. He used to admonish the greedy ones and tell them to give the others a chance.

"When we moved to Cambridge, we found lots of squirrels over in Harvard Yard near the big law building where there is a large grove of oak trees. The old ones respond when you *talk squirrel* to them, and come for nuts, but the young ones seem wary. A good many of the students bring big dogs with them to class. The dogs have to wait outside the buildings for their masters. I suspect that they spend their time then chasing squirrels, and this may have made them shy. I am having a hard time calling them squirrels because we have always called them 'skuggs' like Benjamin Franklin did.

"My husband has reminded me of our best squirrel story. One winter when there was a lot of slush, we gave a peanut to a squirrel on Cambridge Common. He took it and then climbed onto

Maurice's suede loafer—sat there eating the peanut, then went off

quite composedly, as though sitting on a friend's shoe to eat, out of
the puddles and slosh, was quite the thing to do."

Not only is Mrs. K-K an obviously considerate squirrel person,
but an effective linquist in squirrel/skugg parlance.

To show that squirrels do indeed penetrate citadels of lofty cul-
ture other than Harvard Yard, a letter to this effect reached me from
a gentleman in Brooklyn, whose words were these:

"What you told us about adventures and misadventures of the
squirrel in the Big Apple! There's one story that I thought you might
like to add to your personal file on the subject. A friend who works
at the Metropolitan Museum of Art once watched security people
chase one of these frisky creatures all over the European Paintings
Gallery. One of the museum visitors shouted, 'Get a net.' But visits
from the park's residents are not at all rare. A few weeks back I saw a
wren in the Junior Museum."

But before I discuss squirrels in the museum, let me say that in   107 my first article I mentioned that I had seen squirrels that were the black, or melanistic, phase of the gray species in Central Park, and that these variants increased as one went north in the range of the gray. However, I said that I had never seen the white, or albinistic, phase of the gray in the park. Further, despite a careful search of the literature and a questioning of the authorities, I had been unable to come up with any record of one. I was later corrected on this. My informant was Mrs. Katharine Janowitz, who at the time lived on the western side of the park. Her letter stated:

"I am writing to let you know that I have seen an albino squirrel in the precincts of Central Park. This was several years ago and, confirming the research citing entrances as the locale preferred by most of the squirrel population, this rare pure-white member was drowsing in the shrubbery at the East Seventy-ninth Street entrance. I have never seen an albino since, but, as I was able to watch him for several minutes, there is no question but that he was the authentic item.' Like the squirrels the article describes, the albino was not in the least timid, and I have no doubt that you will have other letters confirming his existence and perhaps that of other park albinos.

"Blessings on him and his gray brethren."

I decided in due course that, as a conscientious reporter, I should visit the entrance specified by Mrs. Janowitz and attempt to verify her sighting. My correspondents meanwhile had confirmed a number of appearances of other albinos elsewhere. Two I will note came from New England, well into the preferred range of the melanistics. A woman in Baltimore, Maryland, wrote: "I hope to add a bit of information for you about the albino squirrels you mention. Early this past August in Winchester, Massachusetts, my host pointed out an albino running along his back fence. It was a pinkish white. My friend said he had seen it several times. If you want to go further into this, I know my friend would be glad to discuss it. He is Philip P. Wadsworth, 66 Oxford Road, Winchester."

Ninety miles northwest of Winchester came a communication

from a gentleman who enclosed a clipping, illustrated with a photograph, from the Claremont, N.H./Springfield, Vt. *Eagle-Times*. It was date-lined Claremont and headed "Rare White Squirrel Romps at Marion Phillips Complex." The text continued:

If the famed Marion Phillips Apartments white squirrel is a full albino, he might be in need of a pair of strong glasses.

But wearing glasses wouldn't make him, her, or it any more rare than it already is.

According to Tudor Richards, executive director of the New Hampshire Audubon Society, no spring chicken when it comes to observing animals, he has never seen an albino squirrel.

From a description of the accompanying photograph over the phone, Richards guessed the animal is a gray squirrel but also an incredibly rare full albino.

Albinism is a recessive genetic characteristic which stops the normal production of coloring in hair, eyes and skin.

Residents at the Marion Phillips Apartments have known for a long time that this particular squirrel was something special. Its existence has been recorded in newspapers and it owns a special place in the heart of most all the residents of the city's elderly housing complex.

"I don't call him anything, just Buddy," Mrs. Sam Gardner said this afternoon while throwing the nervous animal peanuts.

It wasn't so nervous as to run away from a strange photographer, however, and posed in several comely attitudes.

"In my thirty years as a wildlife biologist and forester, I

have never seen a full albino squirrel. I've seen stuffed albino porcupines, and other albino animals, but never a squirrel," Richards said in disbelief.

He added that he had seen the reverse of the phenomenon, completely black pigmentation, but never all white.

Human albinos have pink eyes, white hair and milky-colored skin. This squirrel has completely white fur, except for a pinkish colored band down its back, apparently pink eyes, and possibly white skin, although it would have no part of such close-quartered observation.

From his knowledge of human albinos, Richards said he didn't think the squirrel would be greatly affected by his coloring.

"I knew an albino hurdler from Michigan back in the Forties who was very good at the sport, but did have to wear heavy glasses," he said.

Mr. Richards is probably right about albinism being an inconsiderable physical handicap. Living things display the trait widely. Many species of domesticated animals exhibit it. And it is not unknown, as Richards noted, among wild animals—or even in plants. Flowers especially may show it. Once the general assumption was that albino human beings were weaker than their pigmented counterparts, but tests have shown that there is no basis for this belief. Presumably an albino squirrel is as strong as any other.

In an effort to investigate my correspondent's report of an albino squirrel in Central Park, I dutifully went up not long ago to the East Seventy-ninth Street park entrance where she had seen it. It was early on a sunny afternoon. A number of people were on benches there, some of them feeding squirrels. I asked several of the older people, who, I believed, were more likely to know, whether they had any recollection of an albino there. None had. However, a number of years have passed since the albino was glimpsed. Much, even in a short time, can happen to city wild things. Consequently,

I have no reason to question the statement of Mrs. Janowitz. On the basis of her observation then, the presence of at least one albino must be added to the annals of Central Park squirrels.

As this book was going to press, word came to me of another Central Park albino. One of my daughters, Maeve, exercises by running regularly in Central Park with friends who, like her, aspire to careers in the theater. One of these, Roger Grunwald, was with her when on two occasions a week or so apart they saw a pure white squirrel, probably the same animal both times. It was in a section near the Winterdale Arch at about the level of West Eighty-second Street, a couple of hundred yards northeast of the American Museum of Natural History. "It was running about on the turf under the trees," Roger told me. "I said to Maeve, 'There's a white squirrel.' I was quite surprised."

I, too, am quite surprised. But quite happy, also, to get the news.

Since the East Seventy-ninth Street park entrance practically adjoins the rambling menage of the Metropolitan Museum of Art, I went to the public relations people there to inquire whether at the moment they were housing any squirrels. Or, for that matter, other elements of park wildlife. The young man at the desk, somewhat taken aback at my query, made telephone calls to the security forces and to the administration office. He then assured me that at the time of my visit the official position was that the institution was completely free of squirrels and other forms of park wildlife.

Although I didn't doubt the museum's official pronouncement, I was anxious to take a look at the European Paintings Gallery, the squirrel's playground as reported in Mr. Black's letter. Accordingly, I went to the building's top floor, where so many masterpieces from across the Atlantic hang. There were, when I arrived, no squirrels on the premises. But I had not found the news that a squirrel had romped in the museum some time in the past completely unexpected. The squirrel is supremely an indoors/outdoors type, and there are apertures in the museum skylights, and elsewhere, through which an able-bodied squirrel could squeeze.

I turned up no squirrel as I wandered about the exhibition, but there is almost always an inanimate squirrel or two to be found in the museum. They are on picture postcards sold in the card shop on the main floor, in the Great Hall, to the right of the grand staircase. One that I bought was a popular item, I was told: Card Number U 23, entitled "Squirrel in a Hazelnut Tree," a detail from "The Unicorn Is Killed and Brought to the Castle," the sixth tapestry of the series, *The Hunt of the Unicorn*, which is probably Flemish, woven about 1500.

Some paragraphs from a gentleman on the West Coast, part of whose epistle has already been quoted, posed for me what was a very interesting question. The paragraphs began:

"The dreariest teacher I ever had taught Biology I to freshmen. In nine months I made a notebook entry only once.

"That was when he laid on us the way a squirrel cracks a nut.

"This animal, he said, has incisors superficially similar to those of many other animals, parallel and sharp. With these he chews two small holes in a nut. Now the difference. The teeth are 'hinged' and can be moved by the musculature of the lower jaw. He inserts the teeth in the holes and spreads them apart. The leverage so exerted snaps the shell.

"He *said* that, and executed a really elegant blackboard drawing of the mechanics.

"I have queried a number of biologists in subsequent decades. None was an expert in vertebrate anatomy, but they all laughed.

"Could the dreary biologist have been right?"

I took the matter up with two consequential squirrel authorities. Their opinions agreed. The first said, "The lower incisors, longer than the upper, can be moved independently during feeding." The second: "The lower jaw has movement. The lower incisor teeth can be spread apart up to a quarter of an inch."

Thus it appears that the widely ridiculed and now probably dead teacher of freshman Biology I was, in fact, right on.

8.   MORE LETTERS

This chapter, for reasons that will shortly appear, might well be addressed to the International Movement of Squirrel Watchers.

It starts with a note that was one of the more surprising and certainly the most provocative that I received. It concerned an error I had made, quite unknowingly and with scientific sanction, in my first article. The letter came from a schoolchild in Canada, written in large, youthful letters with a red ballpoint pen on blue-lined notebook paper of the sort that is regularly used in elementary classes. It said (reproduced here with the original punctuation): "In the September 9th issue of *The New Yorker*, In the article on Central Park Squirrels, you state that 'Cracked nuts (which would spoil) are never buried' But I have observed, in Toronto, that they do. Why? Jennifer Schengili, age 9, 105 Wineva ave., Toronto Ontario Canada."

I was, in all truth, flummoxed by that imperious "Why?" For I had certainly said, on the basis of considerable research into scientific literature and conversations with zoologists I knew, that squirrels do not bury cracked nuts. However, I was not paralyzed. I called on the telephone, in his office at North Carolina State University, Dr.

F. S. Barkalow, a leading squirrel authority. I relayed Jennifer's announcement. He said that though it is possible for a single squirrel to do almost anything with a nut, in his experience squirrels do not bury cracked ones, thus confirming my original impression. I concluded that Jennifer was perhaps having truck with a passel of squirrel cretins.

This, however, was not the case, as I found out upon further investigation. In the interest of scientific accuracy, I toyed with, but put aside, the notion of racing up to Toronto to see Jennifer and her squirrels. Instead, I decided to call her mother and inquire whether the facts on the nut-burying squirrels were indeed those that Jennifer had reported. In as grave a matter as this, I thought, such new intelligence should not go into the pages of zoology on the mere say-so of a nine-year-old. Mrs. Schengili told me that everything her daughter had said was quite correct. "The squirrels in our northerly area are both grays and the black, or melanistic, form of the grays," Mrs. Schengili said. "We live in a section of town called The Beaches. It is along the lake, and has many squirrels, both gray and black. We feed them all the time, not just with peanuts, but with a mixture of nuts. Some of these are cracked. But we have seen them bury these right along with the sound ones."

That, you might think, would have ended the matter, but I had another thought. If Toronto squirrels bury cracked nuts (which in due course would most certainly spoil), would they by any chance bury nuts without any shell at all, which would certainly spoil much quicker? In the interest of broadening scientific information, I felt this question, too, should be answered. I telephoned in Toronto the office of the Boy Scouts of Canada, whose personnel, I thought, would be not only prepared, but reliable and wise in the ways of nature. Following some initial astonishment by the switchboard operator, expressed by audible gulps into her mouthpiece, at the explanation for my call, she put me in touch with Andrew L. Jackson, the
114   director of the Training and Program Office, a man who knows both

squirrels and The Beaches well. He agreed to get in touch with the Schengilis, with whom I was by then on cordial terms, and conduct my suggested experiment, namely to take some shelled nuts out to their home and see what would happen.

Mr. Jackson's subsequent report is embodied in this letter:

"Sorry about the delay in arranging to meet the Jennifer Schengili squirrels. We finally got all parties together and what an interesting performance.

"Jennifer is a bright, nine-year-old nature lover who attends special club meetings of the Royal Ontario Museum and in the field on nature rambles nearly every weekend.

"The morning I visited her it rained, and there was a crew of men pruning and grinding up the cuttings nearby. What a noise and not much hope in rain to attract squirrels. Jennifer scratched half a walnut on the stonework. Up came Peter, peeked around the corner, bobbed hello, and proceeded to clean out the half shell. Then I got into the act. I fed him shelled unsalted peanuts. He certainly filled himself and we despaired of seeing him bury any. However, after eating six or eight, he ran over to the base of a silver maple, and buried the next three. With the fourth, he performed beautifully. He went two doors north, cleared away the leaves, dug a sizeable hole, laid in the nut, covered it over thoroughly, and then re-arranged the leaves.

"At this point, up came Rings, a gray squirrel, and closed out the performance. He would not allow Peter near us, and then sat in the tree to make sure the act was over.

"Jennifer's squirrel family is made up of other members. There's Mooch, a black; and Beggar, Grabber and Brooch, all grays. Oh, yes, and Rings, an unusual gray with white markings—a most officious individual. They all trust Jennifer and no wonder. She treats them as friends and allows them to lead their own lives. She does not possess them.

"So squirrels do bury raw nuts. And they love peanuts. But they   115 must be unsalted. Thank you for making it possible for me to meet Jennifer's friends. I and my children have fed squirrels and admired them for years, but this crowd of squirrels was great."

Information about Jennifer did not stop with Mr. Jackson's letter. The secretary of the Toronto Field Naturalists' Club, with which Jennifer is connected, wrote me, enlarging on the young lady's activities. He said: "Jennifer is an active member of the Toronto Junior Field Naturalists' Club that meets on the first Saturday of each month and whose leaders also are taking their minerals, snakes, turtles, and telescopes to public libraries around Toronto in order to bring the wonder and beauty of nature to the city's youngsters. We look forward to Jennifer becoming one of the leaders in a few years."

Nor was this all. I received from the author a clipping of a feature story in *The Toronto Star*, illustrated with a photograph of Jennifer corroborating the textual description of her as "a tall, clear-eyed girl with long blonde hair." It might also have added the word "pretty." Among other things, the piece identified the color of Squirrel Peter, a fact omitted in Mr. Taylor's report. Peter is a black. The item included the sad news that some of the squirrel band had gone ape: "Unfortunately," the article went on, "the squirrel feeding days are over, since some of the mob got into the attic, started raising a family, and chewed the roof which had to be re-shingled." But it added that Jennifer makes do with a gaggle of other pets which, at the time, included Jewels, a turtle; Alice and Harry, hamsters; and a tank of tropical fish.

And Jennifer's influence in a salutary way extended far from Toronto. A schoolteacher of Palo Alto, California, wrote me as follows: "Thank you for your articles and for the information that squirrel watchers seem to be everywhere. I underlined the most informative paragraphs, especially about the tail, and read these to my second-grade class. They were quite impressed. I then gave them a project called 'The Frogs of Windy Pond,' and urged them to be as observant as was Jennifer Schengili of Toronto. I would have liked to have put them in touch with her."

Today Jennifer's interest in nature continues. The hamsters have been replaced with gerbils, but Jewels, the turtle, is still a member of the household. And Jennifer now has under consideration the career of zookeologist. This, I was told by Mrs. Schengili, is an ecologist who works at a zoo.

Half a dozen of my communicants, following publication of Jennifer's letter, told me they had seen squirrels burying cracked nuts, unshelled nuts, and even other spoilable foodstuffs, among them a woman from Denver, Colorado, who reported her childhood memories of cracked-nut burying in Brooklyn's Prospect Park, and my friend, Miss Cynthia Westcott, the erstwhile Plant Doctor, who logged in with tales of cookie-burying.

However, I think the most informative response on the subject came from William Russ, of Louisville, Kentucky, obviously an observer whose opinion could be trusted. His letter began:

"I believe there is a difference between a squirrel storing nuts by burial and burying nuts for temporary storage. My experience with one squirrel is all the evidence I have, but I've observed this individual's behavior for nearly five years.

"Stumpy is a female gray whose only notable difference from the other grays in the neighborhood is her short tail. A woman living nearby told me that Stumpy had been around here 'long before you moved here and she's always had a short tail' so I don't know her exact age. She's lost about two-thirds of the appendage and until this summer it's been straight across the tip, like a bottle brush, but this spring a few scraggly hairs have started growing and they curve toward each other at the tips, making a vague, skeleton outline of a rounded tip. She's very easy to identify at a distance because of her appearance, and I've watched her burying peanuts from a few feet away to as far as I can see in any direction. Of course, she disappears from time to time, carrying and burying food even farther away, obviously.

"I began feeding Stumpy about three years ago and she's gradually come closer and closer until she now comes all the way to my

feet to be fed. Although I could have her take food from my hand I think it's better not to begin it, for safety reasons.

"Once or twice a day she'll appear on the sidewalk at the far end of my backyard and come skipping up the walk toward the house, with a little pause-and-sit-up here and there to check for possible danger, until she gets to my screened back porch. She climbs the step and peers through the screen door, and if I'm not in sight she climbs the screen porch walls. She crawls sideways across and around the end of the porch to get as close as possible to the glass door and tries to peer into the house.

"When I come outside, I carry a handful of unshelled peanuts, and prop open the screen door with my left foot. If she has retreated in disappointment but is anywhere in sight I then call her by name. She comes scampering back and as she approaches the house begins a zigzagging course and puts on what I consider is a display of mock fright. She creeps up and runs back a few times before smelling my shoe toe and cautiously climbing the step onto the porch. If any large object on the porch has been moved to a different place since her last trip, she stands back and sniffs at it before proceeding further. I then toss a peanut toward the far end of the porch and she goes after it. When she comes back she prepares to ease gingerly past me to the outside again. At this point I always say, 'Want another one?' She always stops then and looks up inquiringly. I drop another peanut in front of her and she moves peanut number one into one side of her mouth, and works to pick up number two. This is just about all she can manage, although on one occasion I saw her struggle until she got three peanuts into place. Then she runs outside to bury or eat the nuts, depending on her mood.

"I find that feeding peanuts two at a time generally causes her to make five trips to the porch before she's satisfied. If she's not very hungry, she'll make five trips, but the last time she'll bury the remaining two nuts. After that, no amount of calling will bring her back.

"Time after time I've noticed that when I give her a peanut with 119 a split hull she'll stop and eat it before she leaves the porch, or bite a small hole in the shell and carry it outside and eat it. This is practically every time. Sometimes I'll substitute one or two peanut butter crackers. She picks these up, runs outside and begins a combination licking with the tongue and scraping with the teeth to get the peanut butter off the cracker. Then she'll eat all or part of the cracker, or occasionally leave it.

"I bought a package of pine nuts from the supermarket the other day, thinking to give her a treat, but she confounded me by passing them up in favor of peanuts. I experimented twice. In each instance, she picked up one pine nut from a little pile, tasted it, put it down and passed on by to pick up a peanut.

"Many times I've experimentally substituted a food other than peanuts. I've then seen her carry the unusual kind out into the yard, quickly scrape a shallow hole and arrange some grass over it. This is a stash and not a storage burial. She's more interested at the moment in her regular food, and will come back to this a little later.

"She buries all types of food in this way. Bread, crackers, broken-shelled peanuts, pieces of apple, etc. Twice I've given her ears of boiled corn on the cob, which she can hardly carry, and watched from a little distance as she carried these to the top of an evergreen near the garage and wedged them between the trunk and a branch. [As squirrels will also do with small bones on which they gnaw to diminish their incisors.] In a day or two the corn is gone. It's always possible that another squirrel or a bird might find the corn, but I think that Stumpy comes back and eats it at her leisure.

"Whenever she buries a nut for what I consider winter storage, she makes a fairly deep hole and covers over the buried food so tightly and securely that she leaves practically no trace on the surface. On one occasion, after watching her bury a nut in the grass, I went to the exact spot and could find no trace of the burial. She rams the earth back into the hole, using all the power of her strong little haunches, pushing her front end like a little battering ram.

120　　　"Stumpy has buried hundreds of unshelled peanuts in the soft earth beneath two large Norway spruces in my backyard. I'm sure I've never seen her carry off nutmeats and truly bury them. Nor have I ever seen permanent burial by Stumpy of bread, candy or other perishable food. My observation of her leads me to believe that she makes a distinction between a temporary hiding place and a storage site."

Here we have, clearly developed, a condition that I suspect occasionally occurs in science. Researchers, completely engrossed in their personal experiments, neglect the general picture and laymen, using their eyes, fill in the gap. Therefore, on the strength of statements by Jennifer, Mrs. Schengili, Mr. Jackson, and my other correspondents, three new facts can be added about squirrels. Those in The Beaches of Toronto and in a number of other places not only bury nuts with cracked shells, they bury nuts with no shells at all as well as various other food items. Furthermore, what Mr. Russ writes seems sensible to me. Squirrels probably differentiate between short-term and long-term storage. While they may conceal perishable foodstuffs temporarily underground, in all likelihood what they inter for lengthy storage is something that withstands rot.

To justify the international scope mentioned earlier as pertaining to this chapter, let me now give the contents of two more letters from Canadians.

The first tells of an almost unfathomable experience:

"Two years ago at my summer cottage sixty miles north of Lake Ontario, one or more squirrels gnawed through the rubber facings of my car's bumpers, front and rear. More devastating, he (or she or them) gnawed a hole in the rubber hose that provides brake fluid. We did not discover this until the first time, homeward bound, my wife needed to apply the brakes—and there weren't any. Since our summer place is quite remote, we had to undergo the hair-raising experience of driving sixty miles with no other stopping power than the lower gears and the parking brake. And if you drive a car, you know the so-called handbrake is a poor thing as far as stopping is concerned.

"What puzzled me is that the fluid seeping from the gnawed brake hose had a nauseating smell—at any rate, to the human nose. Since then, when we park at the cottage, the car has been surrounded by planks painted with creosote, augmented by a scattering of moth balls. We have suffered no further squirrel vandalism, but I do not feel secure. Any creature that could relish that noxious brake fluid might well regard creosote and moth balls as a sort of canape. I can only conclude that squirrels are more omnivorous than the much-maligned goat that does not really eat tin cans."

This is certainly odd. Since rubber is soft, not hard, and could not be used in lessening incisor length, one assumption is that the couple somehow became involved with one or more of the local crazies.

The second letter came from the Philippine Islands. It said:

"My wife and I have been living in Manila for some time, but our normal residence is in Ottawa, Canada, where we have a home on a well-treed lot which is adjacent to very extensive parkland. We have lots of squirrels. Let me tell you about our psychedelic ones. At our latitude, squirrels must go into semi-hibernation during the winter; at least one doesn't see them during very cold weather. When there is an unseasonable thaw or very late in the winter when the sun is bright and warm, they come out and are everywhere in the bare elm branches.

"At the back of our garden there is a wild honeysuckle bush that was there when the place was in its original condition of bush and pasture. One winter when the squirrels came out in mild weather, they began stripping the bark from this bush. They would cram more and more of it into their mouths and sit, with their cheeks bulging, chomping away. After a certain time they would go wild, with joy apparently. They would rush around, chasing each other, making absolutely impossible leaps from branches, occasionally falling backwards, leaping up, jumping up and down, and rolling over and over in the snow in a pure frenzy of delight. They particu-

larly liked to leap about in the honeysuckle bush itself, running up one branch to the slender end, flinging themselves into the air like acrobats and miraculously landing on another slender branch. This was not the ordinary post-hibernation frolic of a normal squirrel. This was speeded-up action—an extra dimension of ecstasy. They had such a drunken revel that winter that the bush was completely denuded and had to be cut back to the ground in the spring."

Naturally, I sought some satisfactory explanation from botanists, including my squirrel-person friend at Harvard. But none in the East that I talked with were able to help me on this matter of ecstasy-producing wild honeysuckle bark. My Harvard contact did, however, point out that a scientist on the West Coast was particularly knowledgeable about substances that alter behavior, having written a highly regarded book entitled *Narcotic Plants*. I eventually located him at California State University and, over the phone, put the question to him. Giving him time to catch his breath and consult his sources, I called again in a few days. He was, unfortunately, unable to clear up the problem. Not knowing where else to turn, I accordingly leave this conundrum to researchers of the future.

9. ODDITIES

This chapter deals with what I call oddities—incidents or situations concerning squirrels that might strike a person as bizarre, peculiar, or surprising.

First a baker's half-dozen of unexpected acts. A letter from a friend went thus:

"Witness this brutal, wanton, and unprovoked attack by a gray squirrel upon a friendly and certainly innocuous tyke of twelve (me).

"This would be in about 1943, and I was proceeding as slowly as my forthcoming appointment with a dentist would allow across Rittenhouse Square in Philadelphia when I felt a sharp and totally unexpected tug upon the right pant leg. I may have been walking slowly (in fact, I'm certain I was), but I was still progressing, when this occurred. Before I could realize the nature of the problem, the tug had moved up my pant leg, onto my jacket, and up to my shoulder, where, before I even fully realized it, I found sitting quite comfortably a gray squirrel. When I turned my head to the right, I found myself looking directly into its eyes, and it was sitting quite calmly by this time upon my shoulder.

" 'Phhht!' it said, before I had a chance to speak. Or, at least, it sounded like 'Phhht!' And then, 'Phhht!' again.

" 'Phhht!' I thereupon replied. 'Phhht, phhht!' (As I have told you, I was a friendly sort in those days.) The enthroned squirrel and stationary I remained thus, trading 'Phhhts!' for some moments in what I took to be good fellowship, but it is quite possible I said something to offend it. In any case, before I realized it, my new-found acquaintance set out across my face. Perhaps it meant me no harm; I really don't know. I do know, though, it dug its quite sharp front claws into my cheek and eyebrow at the first step. Where it was going I really cannot say (my other shoulder, perhaps?) since fortunately I reached it before it could take another step, and dig its rear claws into me. Disabused, I threw the animal from me. Before the stream of blood from my eyebrow closed the eye, I noticed it landed, apparently quite unhurt, on the branches of a bush, and scampered victoriously away. A few minutes later, I arrived at my dentist's, bleeding profusely from six deep puncture wounds, caused by the beast's claws. The dentist provided the proper antiseptic and dressings. But I don't think he believes to this day my tale of being set upon by a squirrel."

Now two instances of freakish thefts. A while back, a visitor to the Brooklyn Botanic Garden took a closeup shot of a squirrel with a tiny Japanese camera. When he laid it aside to make a record of the shot, the subject, possibly enraged, possibly seeking privacy, dropped down, snatched the camera, and disappeared with it up a tree for good.

As for the second instance, in Bienville Square, a park in Mobile, Alabama, a policeman, M. Marshall, was astounded and offended to see a young man clambering nimbly in the branches of a park tree in ardent pursuit of a squirrel.

"Descend," the officer ordered. The climber complied after first reaching into a lofty crotch for an object. The arboreal adventurer, it turned out, was a visitor from Florida. When he had accidentally dropped his automobile keys on the ground, one of the square's squirrels in a lightning dash had seized them, borne them aloft, and, after a whirlwind chase through the foliage, had deposited them in the woody fork.

On another occasion, secreted goods caused a trip to an auto service station. The owner of a Buick, a car which at that time sported a design with chrome-ornamented circular openings on the sides of the hood, was troubled and puzzled by a mysterious jangle under the hood unlike any vehicular noise he had ever heard before. A minute inspection by the repairman disclosed a cache of acorns in the car's engine compartment, apparently stored there by a squirrel going to and fro through the hood's holes, the inventive animal preferring this type of hoarding to the more traditional one.

And probably just as bemused as the auto owner was the Florida correspondent of an outdoors magazine who wrote of the gray squirrels that he had seen "Marching over the grass—a sedate procession, in which the leading squirrel buried a nut that was dug up in turn by each of his followers; the line reforming itself and reburying the nut till none of us could calculate either how many squirrels would be disappointed, or how many times this would occur, when the season came for harvesting cached food." A mysterious procedure, surely.

Having noted the squirrel in unexpected acts as assailant, thief, innovator, and clown, let us now consider the squirrel as hero, the linchpin in a successful combined effort to rescue a fledgling grackle. The actors in this affair, which occurred deep in the outback of Brooklyn, were a wise old squirrel, a family of grackles and their relatives, a Scotch terrier, two human assistants, and the villain, a rapacious yellow-and-orange cat. The squirrel, well-known in the neighborhood, cadged handouts by pretending physical infirmity, limping about and feigning all sorts of ill health. On this occasion, around noon, when mother grackle was feeding her babies, one fell from the nest onto tree-shaded turf. From nowhere, the cat, notorious as a consumer of baby birds, leaped on the fledgling. Mother and all neighborhood grackles at once set up a concerted racket, audible for blocks. The cat, entirely unconcerned, went over a fence with bird in mouth. Now arrives the hero, craftier, far craftier, than the cat. Often in the past it had evaded the charges of this same predator—though here and there scar tissues on its pelt gave testimony to either the narrowness of its escapes or its lighthearted daring. Down a tree trunk it now comes and sits by the cat. The gluttonous cat regards it voraciously. Squirrel, shamming an obvious limp, moves nearer, almost to within paw length. Squirrel or grackle? ponders cat.

Now a Scotch terrier that hates cat enters. Quickly grasping the situation, it noiselessly races forward while cat is regarding squirrel. Once in range, employing a titanic leap and full-throated barks, it drops all stealth and makes for cat, fangs bared. Utterly surprised,

cat releases grackle and barely gains the safety of a fence, the sneering chatter of squirrel starting to ring in its ears. The terrier's two owners, responding to the racket, come on the scene, pick up the fledgling and restore it to the nest. Squirrel, meanwhile, now up a tree, proceeds to pour forth triumphant obscenities on cat ad infinitum.

Finally, in this baker's half-dozen, consider the eccentric action of a squirrel reported to me by Dr. William B. Willcox, the present editor of the Benjamin Franklin papers, a task that requires him almost every day to enter and leave the Sterling Library at Yale University, where his office is located. Dr. Willcox has his work cut out for him, for Franklin was one of the greatest word producers of all time. So far, despite great industry on the part of Willcox and his predecessors, the published volumes of Franklin's writings number only twenty-odd. Perhaps an equal number are envisioned. One day, as Willcox was hurrying into the library, a tall, imposing Gothic structure located in the heart of the campus, he saw a large cardboard carton slowly but inexorably moving up the ivied wall near the library's entrance, which is set within a lofty, cathedrallike nave. Mesmerized, he watched the box's measured ascent. When it reached the top of the perpendicular surface and moved onto the slanting roof, Willcox discerned the motive power, a highly satisfied gray squirrel. "I'm still wondering," Dr. Willcox told me, "what it intended to do with its captive. Whatever that might have been, I'm sure Ben would have found the episode vastly interesting."

I don't know whether everyone would describe as an oddity a squirrel ingesting beverage alcohol. But I think I would. A woman in a letter to me from San Francisco tells of an experience with a drunken squirrel in Germany. Mrs. Frederick Simon writes: "I would like to add to your interesting file another story, a true one. Some years ago when I still lived in Europe, I had a neighbor who had a house next to mine that bordered on a forest. The house was beautifully furnished with admirable objects of art and embroideries everywhere. A most precious bedspread of Brussels lace covered the bed in the guest room.

"One day entering the guest room my friend found the elegant bedspread torn to pieces. She was wondering who could have done such an ugly job. She asked the servants but none of them could find the answer.

"On the night table, the lady of the house had placed a box of chocolates filled with brandy for her expected guest. In the evening before her guest was to arrive she went again into the room. And what did she find? The box of brandy-filled candies was completely empty and on the lace cover a squirrel was lying, evidently drunk, and laughing as only (she thought) a human being could laugh. Immediately she called the entire staff of the house. Nobody had ever seen a drunken, laughing squirrel before."

But intoxicated squirrels are not confined to Europe. In Wilmette, Illinois, one pursued a postman making his rounds. Reeking of alcohol, it mounted the trouser leg of Mailman Anthony Hermes. The startled postman shook it off. However, the assailant, high as a kite, returned time after time. The letter carrier fled up an alley, the squirrel close behind. Safety was finally gained when the beleaguered sprinter popped into the entrance of a bowling alley and slammed the door shut. Rotting fruit whose sugar had turned to alcohol was the presumed intoxicant. And in an area of northern New Jersey where houses had been plagued for some time with squirrel infiltrators, a homeowner returned to find a squirrel atop his bar guzzling from an overturned bottle of whiskey whose cork it had worked loose—a bottle of imported Scotch, in fact, a natural selection, perhaps, for a quality-minded squirrel.

Nor are odd potables the only things that squirrels consume. Just as odd, possibly even odder, are other things they have eaten. Some mushrooms are great delicacies. But mushrooms can be poisonous. Two of the most lethal are the fly amanita and the destroying angel mushroom. The former, when ingested by a human, paralyzes the nerves that control the heart action; its juices injected into the blood of an anesthetized cat cause death in less than a minute. The destroying angel mushroom of the same family is also highly toxic to human beings. Not so to squirrels, however. Dr. Vagn

Flyger, in an effort to prove this point, collected five hundred pounds of these mushrooms and fed them to some caged squirrels. The result: "The low-calorie diet made them lose some weight," Flyger said. "But they still thrived."

Even more remarkable to me, if true, is what was reported consumed in England by a gray, the word coming from a writer there who enjoys the reputation of being a competent squirrel authority. He wrote: "In Cheshire a squirrel remained steadfast and undaunted eating the remains of a strychnine-poisoned hen carcass while three rats which had also partaken of the food lay dead at his side." It seems almost incredible to me that a squirrel could munch happily away on strychnine, yet here is a record of it. As Dr. Flyger said after his mushroom experiment, "It would be interesting to know how they do it."

It may seem wildly improbable that a physical system that can withstand strychnine and poisonous fungi should be so fine-tuned and delicate as to cause its owner to perish from shock when left overlong in a live trap, but that, science says, is the case with the gray squirrel. Therefore it would probably amount to cruel and unusual punishment for a gray to be jailed for cause in the state of Illinois, where the statutes provide for incarceration of law-breaking animals.

Squirrels on occasion have received money, real coin of the realm, that is, both from employment and from bequest. A big earner was Snoopy, which appeared in more than one hundred motion pictures and earned thousands of dollars. More ordinary creatures, park squirrels in Washington, D.C., received a trust fund in the will of a man; the legacy was in gratitude for the pleasure their gamboling and cavorting had afforded his mother.

Coats of arms in Europe, as might be expected, have featured squirrels in various postures. But there is at least one example of a squirrel on the escutcheon of a notable American family. The Lees of Virginia, descended from Colonel Richard Lee, who arrived in the colony before 1646, have a squirrel on their crest shown cracking a nut.

Among my personal experiences with squirrels, one of the more touching occurred in Harvard Yard by the gate between Lehman and Straus Halls that gives onto Harvard Square, the subway station, and the big newsstand. It was a busy moment on a sunny morning. Classes were changing. Students and faculty, bookbags over shoulders, were thronging in and out of the gate by which I was standing to keep an appointment. On the ground was one of the Yard squirrels, somewhat amused. Only a few yards off was a dog, a pointer, poised in an absolutely magnificent point, tail stiffly directed in a stance that projected an absolute bull's-eye upon the squirrel. Both animals remained in these positions for I don't know how long, the dog increasingly despairing, the squirrel, I suspect, growingly entertained. Perhaps because I feel so close to dogs I sensed keenly the pathos of the scene. Scores of people swirled by, but none, not one, paid any attention. The tableau was real for only the dog, the squirrel, and me. "God," I could virtually hear the humiliated pointer saying, "won't any of you Mensa-types recognize what's going on here?"

Not every state in the union possesses a state animal, as you may, or may not, know. But North Carolina does. It's the gray squirrel.

Here follow two oddities of a somewhat somber stripe. Seventeen firemen, policemen, and ambulance crew members were felled, and an exterminator was killed, in a Long Island house where a cyanide-derivative dust, being used to rid the place of squirrels, apparently formed a toxic cyanide gas. And in a gangster-ordered rubout of a man and his moll that was taking place in an outlying district of New York City, the two gunmen had already dispatched the man and were turning their attention to the girl when they were interrupted by the fierce chattering of a squirrel in the shrubbery behind them. Being merely innocent children of the pavement, completely unacquainted with the varied sounds of wildlife, they took the noises to be those of an unwelcome human observer. Firing hastily into the bushes, they fled, leaving the wounded girl alive but the censorious

132

squirrel dead. As someone remarked later, in addition to murder, the two gunmen could be charged with shooting a squirrel out of season.

The Cinderella legend is an old, old tale. Versions by the score exist. One book that traces their numerous origins lists more than five hundred variants of what was perhaps an ancient Chinese story to start with.

The faithful reader should hardly be surprised to learn that a squirrel has become entwined with one of the variants, the one that we in this country now recognize as *the* Cinderella story. This version was apparently first told in Norman French. In it Cinderella's slipper was made of *vair*, or squirrel's fur, obviously quite a comfy piece of footwear. When the yarn got to England, the word somehow was changed to the homonym, or sound-alike, *verre*, or glass, which, of course, is the material given in our rendition today—hardly a change for the better as far as the poor lass's comfort goes.

The repeated emphasis in my magazine pieces on the importance of the squirrel's tail elicited a reaction from a gentleman in Montana. He wrote for the periodical *Montana Outdoorsman* an article entitled "Tail Tale," a copy of which he sent me under a covering letter:

"Your article about squirrels and the uses of their tails launched me into my research concerning the many ways that animals use their tails.

"Of course, the more one studies such a profound subject, the more curious he becomes. Why, for instance, does a fox need such an elaborate appendage while a bobcat can survive with a mere token? If a horse needs a tail to switch flies, why not a rabbit? An opossum finds it convenient to hang by his, but the pronghorn antelope uses his to say 'Ta, ta' as he disappears over the horizon."

In his article, the author, Mr. D. Roscoe Nickerson, mentions the tails or lack of them in fifteen animals, several of which he treats, as is his privilege, in a peripheral or cavalier fashion. Cows' tails, he says, are fly whisks or defensive weapons against milkmaids; porcupine tails are whackers to imbed quills; squirrel tails are allotted 133 only three of the more than half-dozen functions I specify; beaver tails are warning water-slappers and also mud-slappers for building up the walls of a lodge; peacocks employ their tails for vainglorious display; and "The old saying that a frog's eyes will fall out if picked up by the tail is not founded in fact." Horses, Mr. Nickerson says, eschewing the obvious use, supply tail hairs to fiddlebow makers and magicians; cats' tails are for mesmerizing birds and other prey; those of elephants are for the following elephants in circuses to hang onto; snakes' tails he does not analyze on the ground that it is impossible to tell where one begins; dogs' tails are emotion indicators; the white-tailed deer's is described, again in a humorous vein, as a method to distinguish the animal from the black-tailed deer; kangaroos sit on theirs; the pig has found "no definite use for his"; and "the bedbug has no tail at all, but he gets there just the same."

Because I am incorrigibly chauvinistic about squirrels, I must point out that in none of my correspondent's examples do his animals display any of the splendid virtuosity evinced by the squirrel's tail, the most impressive, relative to its owner's size, of any possessed by a life form with fur. Although he lists three uses of the squirrel's tail, more than that assigned to any other creature, he neglects four others, including the highly civilized use as a napkin.

And lastly in this litany of singularities, comprised of interesting details that may have escaped the attention of even the most fervent members of the National Association of Squirrel Watchers, we must consider the White House and its environs. Without any question, the White House has for decades been an outright hotbed of squirrel activity. And quite naturally so. The three-story sandstone building painted white has eighteen acres of beautifully landscaped grounds provided with lawns, flower beds, trees, and fountains, ideal habitat for the tree-loving, water-loving *Sciurus carolinensis*. In recent times, several Chief Executives or members of their staffs have been personally involved with the gray-coated residents of the stretches outside. During the administration of Harry S. Truman, for example, an appointment was bestowed on a five-year-old boy, Richard Feeney, to act as Official White House Squirrel Feeder, an unsalaried but, I feel, prestigious post. The commission resulted from a chance meeting of Mrs. Truman and Richard, who told the First Lady that the White House squirrels looked scrawny when compared with their fellows in Lafayette Park, the well-known patch of greenery directly across Pennsylvania Avenue from the Executive Mansion. Some years later President Gerald Ford got a letter from Feeney, then a junior naval officer stationed at Norfolk, Virginia, relinquishing his presidential appointment, saying that while he had greatly cherished the post "there comes a time when one must step down." The president gracefully accepted the resignation.

In the 1950s, when President Dwight Eisenhower occupied the White House, he was much given to practicing his golf game on the lawns. In the middle of his first term, cameramen were barred from using the old State Department Building to the west as a vantage spot from which to snap pictures of the President taking his swings on his residential turf. At the same time, a program of exile was announced for the indigenous squirrels. They were to be dispatched to a place where they could not dig up the president's putting green or carry away his golf balls. When word of this became widespread, a bevy of nature lovers began collecting money under the banner of "Save the White House Squirrels Fund"; they were backed by a senator from Oregon. Thereupon (ostensibly) the idea of sending the squirrels into exile was dropped.

However, some years later when the Democrats reoccupied the White House, a political columnist published what he claimed was the true story of this affair, gleaned from leftover private papers of the Eisenhower administration. In these, he said, it was disclosed that the squirrels continued to be deported or liquidated, and that their continued high numbers on the grounds during this period of banishment and extirpation puzzled presidential aides. The columnist also solved the enigma. He said that, at the time, a Washington woman, married to a trap designer and suffering great depredation of her bird feeders at the nimble paws of squirrels, persuaded her husband to fabricate some live traps whose operations were highly successful. The kindhearted man, who knew optimum squirrel terri-   135 tory when he saw it, religiously released his captives every day through the barred iron fence around the White House grounds.

There has always been traffic by squirrels between the White House and Lafayette Park across the street. The great attraction of the park to squirrels is the amount of food provided there by hordes of government employees at noon who, armed with lunch bags and peanuts, stroll the paths or rest on the benches. And these are augmented, of course, by park visitors, also armed with peanuts. As a

consequence, sometimes the park, which is something less than seven acres in extent, accumulates an over-large squirrel population. This then must be reduced. One of these times occurred a couple of years ago, when an estimated 125 squirrels were present where only one-fifth that number, an authority stated, should be. During this time, the squirrels' appetite outstripped the handouts, and the occupants chewed up five thousand dollars worth of bushes, plants, and other assorted floral matter. Action was required. The removal tech-

nique was to plant fourteen open live traps with food around the park. After some days, when the squirrels had got used to the traps, and would not die from shock upon their closure, the traps were set and the squirrels inside were taken to parks on the outskirts of the city, a process that was repeated until the population had reached the desired level.

The most unusual thing I have so far heard about a squirrel and Lafayette Park was told to me by Dr. Barkalow, the squirrel investigator. He said that he once saw there a squirrel with so bad a case of malocclusion—the lower incisors protruded through the upper jaw—that to feed itself it needed to place its head on the ground, open its mouth, and use its molars at the back of the mouth to seize and crack a nut.

In Franklin D. Roosevelt's tenure at 1600 Pennsylvania Avenue, a black squirrel and a white squirrel lived on the grounds at opposite ends. The time of their arrival and their place of origin has never been precisely determined. Nevertheless, their presence was soon widely known and much commented on by out-of-town visitors and local people. The popular name of the white squirrel became Snow White. From time to time, in feature stories, the capital's papers would describe Snow White as an albino, a characterization that offended somebody in the White House, perhaps Eleanor Roosevelt, an able worker for feminine rights. At any rate, the White House publicly allowed, through an assistant to Presidential Secretary Stephen Early, that the term was repugnant, "a slur on a noble sisterhood."

With such interaction in modern times between squirrels and recent presidents, one wonders about their predecessors. Hoover, Coolidge, Wilson, Taft, Teddy Roosevelt—what of them? And such earlier ones as Cleveland, Grant, Johnson, even crusty old Andy Jackson—did they have traffic with White House squirrels? The squirrels, for their part, were certainly there. The records, if examined, may disclose something along this line. I'll leave the task to historians of the future.

138

10. ANSWERS

Many of my letters contained questions and misconceptions. Taking the misconceptions first, let us look at the very prevalent notion about warfare between the reds and the grays. Several people reported serious, continual strife between the species, not only here but in Great Britain also. Some correspondents gave the grays, some the reds as the invariable victors. For example, a woman living in the town in New Hampshire that is the site of Dartmouth College said: "Concerning squirrels, we have both red and gray in Hanover. The grays are much more visible and quarrelsome than the reds—fighting, scolding the cat and birds, giving each and everyone in sight their informed opinions. BUT THEY DO NOT KEEP THE RED SQUIRRELS AWAY!"

A second correspondent from another part of New Hampshire wrote: "About red and gray squirrels being in competition, I have always heard that the reds will drive out the grays, and in their fights will get the better of the grays. Two days ago, a red chased a big fat gray up one tree, across the roof of my home, down a lilac bush and out of the yard."

This is the kind of contradictory evidence to be found among squirrel watchers. To further emphasize the conflicting views, the New Hampshire gentleman wrote that reds come into his house and create havoc but the grays do not. While the woman, on the other hand, reported that reds and grays in harmony use the same arboreal route to her attic and coexist there.

Evidence concerning red/gray interaction is least burdened with dissent when it comes from Great Britain. There, generally speaking (but not always), the larger gray chases out of the area it wishes to control the smaller and more passive red. In this country, the red, although again the smaller, is far more fiery and is often seen successfully ousting a gray from a piece of territory. Scientific opinion is that the winner of the confrontation is the one that most strongly believes it is the rightful possessor of the real estate on which the skirmish is taking place. And, as far as the gravity of the encounter goes, one of the most experienced of present-day naturalists says he has never seen a serious fight between the two species. When territoriality is not an issue, the two species appear to live peaceably together.

The same seems to be true, in general, when two gray males meet during the mating season, a time when some of those who wrote me reported furious tussles or, more frequently, tales of the tussles received from others. Zoologists generally hold that wild chases and face-to-face meetings in which vituperation plays a large part are standard procedures in determining which male gives ground. However, in the very rare case, I am prepared to believe that an all-out fight may develop in which teeth as well as claws would be used. But that, I suspect, would be the exception.

Another widespread misconception is that reds and grays interbreed. Some of the wildest statements about this come from England. An outraged sportsman in Hertfordshire reported that not only does the mésalliance occur but that "The resultant crossbreed is an animal larger than either of the parents, colored gray with a broad band of red on the back, and combining the vices of both races with the impudence of *Sciurus carolinensis.*" Another Englishman stated that "Interbreeding has turned all reds to grays." One of my Harvard correspondents wrote that the gray squirrels in the Yard have rusty-colored backbone fur. This characteristic occurring there, and elsewhere, including gray tints in red squirrels, has caused several of my correspondents to inquire about interbreeding. It does not take place. The red tones in a gray squirrel and the gray ones in a red are color deviations that are inherent in the stock, the most extreme instances of which are the melanistic and albino phases of both species of squirrels.

By far the commonest misconception, embedded prominently in a score of letters, is that males of the two species castrate the loser in a fight. Sometimes the red, sometimes the gray is named as the castrater. The error is many years old and deeply ingrained in the public consciousness. There is, as a matter of fact, an understandable basis for the belief. People see squirrel chases. A hunter then bags a male and finds no testes in the scrotum. He concludes, and spreads the word, that the quarry has been castrated in a fight.

The testes are not present for a good anatomical reason, explained below. In addition, the scrotum may show a hole through which the larva of the bot fly, a parasite, has emerged, a circumstance that does not, however, harm the squirrel's reproductive powers. The testes are normally lodged in the abdomen except during mating season, a non-hunting period, but can be shaken down. Perhaps the tenacity of this error's hold on the public mind can be illustrated by a story told me by a scientist. He knew a hunter whom he had long tried to convince that squirrels do not castrate one another. To instruct the scientist otherwise, the hunter persuaded him to come with him into the field in the open season. The hunter shot a male and showed it to the scientist. Sure enough, its testicles were not in the scrotum. "Now, will that persuade you?" said the hunter. The other took the corpse and gave it a shake, whereupon the testes descended. "There are the testicles," said the scientist. "Will that persuade *you*?" But the hunter was obdurate. "You keep to your belief," he said. "I'll keep to mine."

Now to the queries.

A couple of readers, obviously pro-squirrel, asked if these charming little creatures ever descend to such barbarous acts as the consumption of birds' eggs and fledglings. The answer is yes. But the required conditions must be met. A large population of squirrels must be present in an area whose customary food supplies have run low. Then the squirrels turn to other forms of sustenance. When normal fare is normally to be found, squirrels show no interest in nesting birds.

A lady in New Jersey asked, "Did Benjamin Franklin originate the term 'snug as a bug in a rug'? My father used to use the phrase all the time." Yes, Ben was the originator of this phrase which was used in his letter containing the epitaph for Mungo, the squirrel.

A gentleman in the sovereign state of Idaho talked about having seen American-looking grays in South Africa, and asked if they were our stock. Yes. The empire-builder, Cecil Rhodes, at the turn of the century, released some of the descendants of American grays in Britain in the Cape Province and before long they took hold in a substantial way. Introductions of grays have also been made in Australia and British Columbia.

What about a collective noun for squirrels, a reader wanted to know. There are, of course, many colorful ones for many other animals—a pride of lions, a gaggle of geese, a band of gorillas, a clutter of cats, a down of hares, and so on. Being unable to locate one for squirrels in my sources, I turned to the editorial staffs of two unabridged dictionaries. After gravely consulting their files over several days, they, too, came up empty-handed. Perhaps, however, another one of my readers has a humorous option—a squawk of squirrels.

Do squirrels have sweat glands, a gentleman wished to know. Or are they, like dogs, lacking them? No, they possess sweat glands; they are located between the toes.

142

A woman in upstate New York wrote what she thought might be a possible explanation for squirrels chewing lead cables: "I remember reading of a medical doctor, who wondered why children ate lead-based paint, tasted it and found it sweet. Perhaps the taste buds of squirrels and the doctor coincide. Do you think so?" No, fair correspondent. Although lead-based paint tastes sweet, the metal does not.

Speaking of taste, a gentleman who subscribes to a natural history magazine pointed out to me that one of its writers hailed the squirrel as possessing the planet's most ironclad digestive tract, far superior to that of the goat. He said that he read that a squirrel digs up and eats daffodil bulbs, which are poisonous, and also cracks apricot seeds and chews up the raw kernels containing a deadly toxin, prussic, or hydrocyanic, acid. How, he wonders, do they survive? Their unusual metabolic abilities, which have been described earlier, are in all likelihood the reason. It might be added, however, that they don't eat the nuts of the horse chestnut, a poisonous seed, especially so when fresh. They shun it, apparently, because they don't like its taste rather than to avoid its dangerous ingredient. After the first bite, they leave it alone.

A reader asked if it would be possible for a squirrel to climb an upright naked house wall, as was reported to him by a neighbor. "How ever could they accomplish this?" he wanted to know. Well, squirrels, as I hope this book has demonstrated, can do highly implausible things. One reader wrote me that he and his wife in New York City's Greenwich Village were continually entertained by watching a squirrel cross a roof and climb down the brick front of an apartment house across the way "to pick up goodies left on the fire escape." And there is an account in a book written by two squirrel authorities of a gray that would climb up the forty-foot side of a tall old house with pebbled exterior to reach an entry hole under the eaves. It progressed by rising at a walking pace, the legs spread a little to each side.

"Where do squirrels go when they die?" a woman asked me.   143

"While I have seen many live ones, I have never seen a carcass." There are, of course, dead squirrels to be seen on roads—highway kills—and these can be numerous during migrations. But it could well be that someone living in a secluded area could see many live squirrels, but none that had died of natural causes. A scientist I asked about this said he believed a squirrel, feeling the end was near, would seek a retired spot in which to lie down and expire.

"Dear Mr. Kinkead: Have you ever heard of a squirrel ghost? I have heard of other animal ghosts. Are there squirrel ones?" I was glad to be asked that question, because I meant to explore every cranny of the squirrel world. Also I am interested in parapsychology. Yet oddly, perhaps, on my own, I had never before this query con-

sidered a squirrel ghost. Why not, I reasoned. Accordingly, I asked the secretary of the Society for Psychical Research in London, and that of the American Society for Psychical Research in New York City, those being the two parapsychological associations to which I belong, whether their files or records held mention of a squirrel ghost, red *or* gray. After a dutiful search, both parties, I regret to say, reported in the negative. Thus, while there are, indeed, records of apparitions of dogs, cats and horses, I and my helpers have been unable to turn up any phantoms of squirrels.

A friend told one of my correspondents what the latter considered an unlikely tale. The friend said that she had finally solved the problem of getting a troublesome squirrel out of her attic by laying a trail of nuts down the stairs and out the front door. "Would this really work?" I was asked. Yes, it would—or could. My wife, in fact, knew of another almost identical case. In that instance, the woman involved put in a hurried call to her grocer, demanding immediate delivery of a pound of assorted shelled nuts. These she cannily used to tempt a highly confused squirrel from the interior of her grand piano.

"Squirrels play games with each other, I know, because I see this. Do they also play games with other animals, as friendly dogs do with some cats?" Yes, this does happen occasionally. One instance was reported from New York State in which a litter of young squirrels, raised in a yard tree, played each summer evening with a young cottontail rabbit at the back of the lawn, seemingly to the great enjoyment of all participants.

A gentleman wrote me, saying, "Considering all that you write about squirrels, I am not sure I wish to be considered a squirrel person. However, perhaps you can answer a question about the tribe. While I was watching television in the dimness of my living room one dark day, a squirrel bumped his nose several times against the window. What was he doing, checking the entertainment scene?" I think not, sir. In all likelihood, he wanted what I suspect another one wanted when a somewhat similar experience happened to me. I was   145 in my darkened office, typing one early afternoon, a gooseneck lamp giving illumination as it was bent over the machine. It was in the month of January, a foul, windy day with freezing rain descending. Outside my office window is a grape arbor a couple of feet from the pane, an easy hop to the windowsill. Several times a squirrel leaped from the bare vine to the sill and batted its nose against the transparent barrier. When I finally made my presence known by moving, it scampered away. I think that it thought it could get in to a cozy, deserted cubicle and find warmth by entering through a clear space which it read as being an opening, not glass.

A friend, a barrister of enormous competence in the field of contracts and money management, is someone who, like so many others, is beguiled by squirrels. He has an original cast of mind, as his letter shows. "Why wouldn't it be a good idea," he wrote, "to do the following to solve the toupee problem for bald elderly men? Graft onto their scalps the pelts of gray squirrels. This would match the color of the fringe of gray hair lower down and the fur, being short, would never need a haircut." Alas, for all my friend's professional skill, and his admirable wish to increase the happiness of elderly baldings, he has evidently failed to have heard of the human body's rejection of alien biological matter grafted onto it.

Lastly, a young lady—a very young lady, I would think—wrote me about the part in Beatrix Potter's story of Squirrel Nutkin in which the protagonist raises its tail as a sail and floats wind-borne across a piece of water on a fragment of wood. "Do you think that really happened?" she inquired. I must doubt that the incident came from Miss Potter's personal experience. It is a situation, however, well-known in folklore. Its origins go back at least to the sixteenth century, when mention of it seems first to have appeared on the printed page. Perhaps Miss Potter was familiar with this reference. Or perhaps she simply used her imagination. In any event, the early European naturalist Olau Magnus is quoted as saying in the middle of the sixteenth century that the squirrel on a piece of wood uses his tail as a sail to get across bodies of water. And the same idea crops up again, somewhat later, on this side of the Atlantic. It appears in a tale heard from an Indian in North Carolina in 1728 by William Byrd. Byrd wrote: "He said whenever the little animal has occasion to cross a body of water, he launches a chip or piece of bark into the water, on which he embarks, and, holding up his tail to the wind, he sails over very safely. If this is true, it is probable men learnt at first about the use of sails from these ingenious little animals." Thus if squirrels were up to this trick in prehistoric times (as they have been said to have been a few centuries ago), it may very well be correct that they gave man the idea for sailboats and that, in addition to this gift to *Homo sapiens*, still another use of their tail may be recorded.

ABOUT THE AUTHOR

Eugene Kinkead has written for The New Yorker *magazine since 1932. He has won two Westinghouse Science Writing Awards, the latest in 1972. His most recent book is* Wildness Is All Around Us. *He lives in Colebrook, Connecticut.*